Anonymous

Religious Thought in Germany

Anonymous

Religious Thought in Germany

ISBN/EAN: 9783337131104

Printed in Europe, USA, Canada, Australia, Japan

Cover: Foto ©ninafisch / pixelio.de

More available books at **www.hansebooks.com**

RELIGIOUS THOUGHT IN GERMANY.

REPRINTED BY PERMISSION FROM "THE TIMES."

LONDON:
TINSLEY BROTHERS, 18, CATHERINE ST., STRAND.
1870.

PREFATORY NOTE.

THE following sketches were originally published in "The Times." They have been carefully revised, and augmented by material additions. Reference in some of them being made to the Letters to the Editor elicited by this Correspondence, the authors of these communications will kindly excuse the appended reprint of their valuable comments.

BERLIN, *May* 26, 1870.

CONTENTS.

CHAPTER	PAGE
I.—THE SCHLEIERMACHER CENTENARY	1
II.—CHURCH AND SCHOOL IN PRUSSIA	9
III.—ANTI-SYLLABUS MEETING	18
IV.—AN ASSASSIN IN THE BERLIN CATHEDRAL	21
V.—THE PRUSSIAN CLERGY	33
VI.—A BERLIN CONVENT	44
VII.—THE GERMAN PROTESTANT ASSOCIATION	58
VIII.—THE BERLIN CONVENT	81
IX.—PROTESTANT ASSOCIATION MEETING.—I.	92
X.—PROTESTANT ASSOCIATION MEETING.—II.	101
XI.—THE HUMBOLDT CENTENARY	109
XII.—A DAY OF PRAYER AND HUMILIATION	123
XIII.—THE PRUSSIAN GOVERNMENT AND THE ESTABLISHED CHURCH	125
XIV.—THE SCHOOLS AND THE ESTABLISHED CHURCH	135
XV.—THE SYNODS	146
XVI.—THE TRIAL OF CARL BILAND	152
XVII.—THE LUTHER MONUMENT AT WORMS	158
XVIII.—THE ŒCUMENICAL COUNCIL	169

CHAPTER	PAGE
XIX.—EPISCOPAL HERETICS	175
XX.—THE GERMAN BISHOPS AND THE ŒCUMENICAL COUNCIL	178
XXI.—GERMAN OBJECTIONS TO INFALLIBILITY AS ADVOCATED BY THE SPANISH, ITALIAN, AND ORIENTAL BISHOPS	189
XXII.—MORE GERMAN OBJECTIONS TO INFALLIBILITY	205
XXIII.—THE FREEMASONS AND THE ŒCUMENICAL COUNCIL	214
XXIV.—AN ANTI-PAPAL MOVEMENT	222
XXV.—GERMAN BISHOPS COMMENTING UPON THE RELIGIOUS MOVEMENT	229
XXVI.—RATIONALISM, CATHOLICISM, AND THE POPE	236
XXVII.—PRUSSIA AND THE POPE	242
XXVIII.—PROBABLE RESULTS OF THE COUNCIL	246
XXIX.—COMING TO TERMS	253
XXX.—THE BAVARIAN ULTRAMONTANES.—I.	260
XXXI.—THE BAVARIAN ULTRAMONTANES.—II.	266
XXXII.—INCREASING OPPOSITION	273
XXXIII.—LATEST ASPECTS	280

APPENDIX :—

A.—LETTERS TO THE EDITOR, TOUCHING THE STATE OF THE PROTESTANT CHURCH IN GERMANY	287
B.—DOCUMENTS RELATING TO THE ŒCUMENICAL COUNCIL	305

LETTERS ON THE STATE OF RELIGION IN GERMANY.

CHAPTER I.

THE SCHLEIERMACHER CENTENARY.

IN all the capitals and universities of Germany the centenary of Schleiermacher's birthday has been celebrated by speeches, liturgies, and the performance of sacred music. The solemnities, originating with what may be called the moderate Liberal party in the cause of religious reform, were equally disapproved by the orthodox and the Anti-Christians; the former of whom protested against, while the latter contented themselves with ignoring, the proceedings. This controversy between the believers and latitudinarians, as well as the significant silence observed by the avowed infidels, alike illustrate the religious condition of the country. Schleiermacher, whose theological teachings were dominant at Berlin in the first quarter of this century, was a man of superior and varied talents, who, if he had not become an eminent preacher, would have equally excelled as a poet, a scholar, and, perhaps, as a minister of state. In fact, in two of these capacities he distinguished himself even while devoted to the service of the church, being one of the most elegant philologists and accomplished philosophical and miscellaneous writers of his day. As a clergyman, his searching mind, combined with a deep and devout religious sentiment, made him the founder of a new school of divines. Yearning for some indissoluble tie to bind him to the invisible world, still too deeply imbued with the sceptical lore of his country to accept the literal inspiration of Holy Writ, he endeavoured to effect a compromise between the two as yet irreconcileable extremes of rationalism and belief. In this, it is true, he only did what so many attempted before, and indeed simultaneously with, him. If he, nevertheless, acquired a loftier position than any of his like-minded cotemporaries, he was indebted for it not only to his immense talent, which would have commanded attention under any circumstances, but also to his differing from other leading ecclesiastics in one particular and most important trait of his intellectual character. The great feature in the man was the reluctance he felt, at least, in some periods of his life, to pronounce peremptorily on the things of the other world. Had he had to deal with matters of mere mundane interest, his want of decision might have been thought a fault;—in a question of such transcendental magnitude, and which was then even more unsettled than now, his halting appeared to his countrymen as incontrovertible proof of modesty, honesty, and singleness of heart. In all that concerned the dogma he never concealed that he wished to be looked upon as an humble seeker after truth. Neither praising nor condemning other more assured minds, he avowed his inability to understand, yet ever acknowledged his duty to adore, the Divine. His very first pamphlet indicated the mediatory office he had taken upon himself. Though written in a spirit orthodox people now-a-days regard as heretical, it was expressly composed to convince the heretics of the last century of the necessity of religious faith. In after life he became more orthodox, though not without relapsing, every now and then, into trains of thought to be understood only if interpreted as in keeping with the predominant liberal convictions of his earlier days. He died a sincere believer, praying to have the Lord's Supper administered, and admitting that it was only through the blood of Christ that he could hope to enter heaven. This occurred some thirty years ago; and in the political turmoil which has since supervened, his memory has been all but effaced from the mind of the masses. Only a small circle, and they highly cultivated men, have never ceased cherishing his name. Holding the opinions propounded by him in the more liberal stage of his life, and wishing to preserve to their countrymen the theistic principles inherent in Christianity, these champions of Schleiermacher have always regarded him as the forerunner of a coming ideal renovation of the Church. The very fact of his adhering to different views in different stages of his religious life, made him the more fit to be set up as an intellectual leader and prototype by the moderate rationalists of the present day. Men, who are opposed to the ancient teaching of the Church, yet have omitted to develop a new and consistent rule of belief, naturally look up to one whose name is identified with a tendency rather than a system. Of the opportunity afforded by the centenary of his birthday they, accordingly, availed themselves to place his career again before the public, and make converts to his general principles. Besides publishing upwards of thirty books, some of them pamphlets, others voluminous biographies of their revered teacher, they arranged festal meetings in the more important towns, representing him everywhere as the apostle of a liberal, yet religious, creed, and one of the greatest thinkers of the age.

To these proceedings the orthodox demurred for a variety of reasons. In the first place, they denied the latitudinarians had any right to regard Schleiermacher as their own, asserting him to have been orthodox rather than otherwise. They also denounced the commemoration as an attempt of the few avowed rationalists among the clergy to extol infidelity under the pretext of doing homage to a defunct genius. And they, therefore, cautioned the ecclesiastical authorities against taking part in, or lending their countenance to, an ovation neither worthy of the man it was destined to celebrate, nor calculated to exercise a beneficial influence on the public mind.

But the Liberals retorted that the orthodox only objected to the commemoration, because, while unable to deny the intellectual eminence and sincere religious devotion of Schleiermacher, they were yet convinced in their heart of hearts, that the man was a latitudinarian rather than one of themselves. In any case, the Liberals were not to be diverted from their object by orthodox criticisms. Zealously continuing their preparations, they asked in Berlin, and, I believe, in some other cities, too, for the churches to be thrown open on a week-day, for the contemplated solemnities. Stout refusals being repeatedly given them by the church authorities, they threatened to petition the king, when the Supreme Ecclesiastical Board, dreading to appear to be opposing not only Schleiermacher's friends, but the memory of the great divine himself, at length gave in, and placed the sacred edifices at their disposal. We have, consequently, had solemn celebrations in the churches, consisting of sermons and hymns, and less ceremonial ones out of the churches, in halls, and private localities, where speeches were delivered, and opinions exchanged, on subjects, religious and political, connected with the life of the eminent clergyman. At the Berlin meeting many of the most renowned followers of Schleiermacher assembled from all parts of Germany to address a numerous and select audience on the merits of their spiritual predecessor. It was really an imposing spectacle to witness, and was sensibly felt to be so by most present. Yet, if it be asked whether it will produce any lasting effects, it would be impossible to answer this question in the affirmative. The truth is, that the majority of the audience, as, indeed, the majority of the educated in Germany, hold more extreme opinions than even the most advanced among the ministers of the Church, who conducted the solemnity, and their small retinue of moderate rationalists. Before they can acquire an interest in such a man as Schleiermacher, the cultivated classes of this country must be won back to the consciousness that religion is a blessing in itself, and that though its ancient forms may not be entirely in unison with the scientific and intellectual development of the era, yet enough of the truth remains to make the kernel worth having when stripped of its shell. Had not the men who arranged the jubilee been eminent in themselves, and were it not considered a gracious and becoming thing to do homage to departed intellectual heroes, it is probable that the public would have taken very little interest in the occasion. Indeed, even as it was, a large portion held back, on the ground that Schleiermacher, after all, was but a clergyman, though, perhaps, a shade less bigoted than his brethren.

The Crown Prince and Crown Princess, who are now staying on your side the Channel, evinced their sympathy in the event by addressing the following telegram to the Burgomaster and Town Council of Berlin :—

"Away from home, we desire to give the Burgomaster and Town Council a proof of our sympathy in the celebrations of this day. The name of Schleiermacher, a man who resuscitated the dormant energies of the Church, and gloriously shared in the revival of patriotic enthusiasm at a time of sore trial [1806-1813], deserves to be had in everlasting remembrance by our people.

"Friedrich Wilhelm.
"Victoria.

"Windsor, November 21, 1868."

This telegram was joyfully received, and is regarded as a most gratifying proof that the interests of the Church and intellectual enlightenment, which, in a healthy state of society, should be identical, are equally cherished by the heir and heiress to the throne.

Berlin, November 28, 1868.

CHAPTER II.

CHURCH AND SCHOOL IN PRUSSIA.

"ONCE upon a time there was a boy named Vitus. He was a good boy, and used to say his prayers every morning as soon as he got up. One morning he forgot to do so, and ran off to school without thinking about it. On the stairs he slipped, fell, and hurt himself. He picked himself up again, and while passing a butcher's shop was again precipitated to the ground by the butcher's dog. An old woman who saw the mishap helped him up, and told him to leave off crying. 'I am sure,' she added, 'you have not said your prayers this morning. Take my advice, go home, undress, go to bed again, say your prayers, and then go to school.' The boy did as he was bid, and when making his way to school for the second time met with no accident. Never after did he forget to say his prayers before leaving his bed."

Thus runs a story in a *Primer* which the Prussian Minister of Ecclesiastical and Educational Affairs has recently forced upon the elementary schools in Hanover. The outcry raised by the inhabitants of the new province at having the doctrine of miraculous interference thus inculcated in the youthful mind eventually induced his Excellency to modify the order introducing the objectionable book into the schools. Still, numerous books conceived in a similar spirit remain.

"Almighty God, I am content to remain the dog I am. I am a dog, a despicable dog. I am conscious of revelling in sin, and there is no infamy in which I do not indulge. My anger and quarrelling are like a dog's. My envy and hatred are like a dog's. My abuse and snappishness are like a dog's. My robbing and devouring are like a dog's. Nay, when I come to reflect upon it, I cannot but own that in very many things I behave worse than the dogs themselves."

So commences a hymn in a church hymn-book recently forced by the same Minister upon certain Protestant congregations in the old provinces of Prussia. And this specimen of its contents is by no means the worst that might be cited. There are some, in fact, too gross to be reprinted. It was only when some of the congregations so treated by the Minister threatened to give up church-going altogether, that the book was withdrawn in their case. Others, more indifferent to what they are made to sing, continue to assert their canine propensities in the sacred edifice.

The number of those attending Divine service is, now-a-days, too small in Prussia to admit of any injunction of the ecclesiastical authorities, however opposed to the feelings of the laity, easily giving rise to a popular movement. The teachings, also, which Protestant parents in this country impress upon their children, as to the manner in which the world is governed, are too universally accepted by public opinion to make them care for anything to the contrary that may be told their offspring in the schools. There are, indeed, plenty of orthodox individuals— nay, even some orthodox districts—to be found in Prussia; but the vast majority of the Protestant middle classes, and even a large portion of the lower strata of society, are estranged from the religion of their ancestors, and take no interest in the Church or the religious lessons thrust upon the schools by Church and Government combined.

If, notwithstanding this prevailing indifference, an attempt at earnest opposition has been recently made in Parliament, in meetings, and the Press, to the ecclesiastical authorities, this is mainly owing to the resolute disregard of public opinion with which orthodox tendencies are being pursued by the Minister and his associates. It is a remarkable fact, that the more rampant unbelief has become among the people, the more strictly is belief professed by the leaders of the Church. Within the last twenty years this contrast has annually increased; and, little as the people suffer from it individually, they regard the latest attitude of the Church as an implied affront. It is true the doctrines with which the children, by order of the Government, are imbued in church and school do not, in this second half of the 19th century, sink very deep into the intellectual system; yet the parents are shocked at seeing their progeny made to learn by heart that for which they themselves have long lost all taste and appreciation. There is another and even worse circumstance connected with the present *régime*. Many of the parents cannot bring themselves to believe that the clergy and teachers believe what they teach. People are ready to admit that there may be some religious enthusiasts adhering to what are now-a-days regarded as antiquated notions; but they refuse to believe that, as a whole, the clergy and teachers of the present day, whose actions apparently proceed from the same motives as those of the common herd, can hold different opinions from themselves concerning the relation between God and man. They are the more prone to doubt the sincerity of the professions made by the clergy, remembering as they do that, from 1815 to 1840, when the Government was virtually latitudinarian, a very large proportion of the pastors were likewise lax in their views. They, therefore, may be frequently heard ascribing the change of opinion which has lately occurred in the Church to the circumstance that those who serve at the altar are dependent upon those who represent the occupant of the throne. Were there anything wanting to confirm them in this malicious imputation, it would be supported by the coincidence, often animadverted upon, that the orthodox majority of the clergy in politics invariably count among the unquestioning supporters of the Government. In the eyes of the public there is a direct connexion observable between Conservatism and orthodoxy. Government have become orthodox since the beginning of the struggle for constitutional rights; the preachers turned Conservative at about the same period. Hence, it is irreverently inferred that the political and religious movement going on among the laity has cemented an alliance between those whose interests seem to require that the ancient forms of subordination to God and the powers that be should be maintained. I need not add that the conclusions drawn from this are equally prejudicial to both Government and clergy.

But, notwithstanding their prevalence, these aspersions on the character of a considerable portion of the clergy are false. To those who have had opportunities of becoming acquainted with the reasonings and feelings of the parties accused, their conduct appears in a more favourable light than popular disparagement will have it. Latitudinarian prejudice may be unable to understand the existence of faith in others, but this is no reason why the faith should not exist. There may, indeed, be hypocrites among the clergy, desecrating religion from a divine into a political instrument. There may be some fighting on the ecclesiastical side who meet latitudinarian antagonism with intrigue, asperity, or haughty contempt of the intellectual attainments of a civilized age. Others, again, attached to canine poetry, may be unable to distinguish between the coarse taste of the seventeenth century—when those hymns were composed—and the more delicate refinement which has since penetrated even to the lower sections of society. But the majority of the pastors are actuated by nobler motives. Loose as their notions may have been thirty years ago, their conversion is not the less sincere because it sprung from the terror they eventually experienced at the lengths to which latitudinarianism went. The revival of the ancient convictions in the Church is simply the consequence of the luxuriant growth of opposite notions in the laity. The preachers who in Protestant Germany were dragged along by the current of popular opinion from 1740 to 1840 were frightened at last to see how far they had been led, and saved themselves by swimming to the shore. The stream had carried them to a cataract, and they effected their escape just in time. Slowly, but surely, advancing in its self-assigned course, public opinion, from impugning the truth of Biblical History, had come to deny by degrees the necessity, the probability, and the possibility of miracles. It now has reached the extent of negativing the efficacy of prayer, and with it the interference of the Almighty in the course of events. It would be useless to waste words on the deep and terrible chasm which this daring assumption creates between the convictions of the present and past. It would lead us also too far to enumerate the reasons alleged to prove that a rational contemplation of the universe as well as a sublime notion of God's nature equally forbid us to believe in His intervention in the daily occurrences of life. But one thing is certain. Were Germany destined to see the notions current among her educated classes accepted by Church and School, this would involve an intellectual revolution of an audacity and comprehensiveness never before witnessed in the world. It would imply the assertion, that whatever may be in store for us in another world, man is supreme in this. It would be the resolve to order this world by the light of reason alone. Suppose these tenets to be recognized by the established powers, to whom is confided the care of political, religious, and intellectual interests, will there be many left to acknowledge the existence of a Divinity and a world to come? True, the existence of a Divinity and a world to come are not necessarily denied even by those assuming that the One has laid down once for all the laws by which the world is governed, and that the other is a sealed book; but the line separating the modern convictions of the Germans from even more extreme views is such a delicate thread that many among the more moderate latitudinarians can realize the emotions with which the orthodox party look upon the whole thing. And in a tightly-governed country like this, who can wonder that the Government should attempt to stem the tide the course of which it disapproves, and the ultimate issue of which it fears? For the present, however, its exertions are as vain as they are easily accounted for. Amid the deafening din of politics, the latitudinarian stream flows silently on, threatening some day to inundate its banks, and change the face of the land more effectually than could be done by any merely political revolution.

BERLIN, *March* 5, 1869.

CHAPTER III.

ANTI-SYLLABUS MEETING.*

AT Worms, the city where Luther, centuries ago, made a solemn declaration of faith, three hundred delegates from the Protestant Societies of Germany have met to vote an uncompromising protest against the Pope, his syllabus, and his endeavours to enforce his antiquated pretensions at the coming Œcumenic Council. The resolutions passed by the assembled three hundred are as strong as they well can be, denouncing in beautifully direct language all hierarchical aspirations, and exposing the demonstrative and not very charitable spirit that has lately manifested itself at Rome. They call the Jesuits the eternal enemies of intellectual culture and progress, represent them as the now dominant party in the Catholic Church, and solicit the assistance of all Germans, both Catholics and Protestants, to wage war against an institution so opposed to the best feelings of the nation and the enlightened

* A translation of the Syllabus is given in the Appendix.

spirit of the age. No less than twenty thousand people were present at the solemn announcement of these modern theses in the market-place of Worms. Loud was their applause, and full and joyous the chorus that sang Luther's " Feste Burg" at the close of the ceremony. There is, indeed, no doubt that the immense majority of educated men in this part of the Continent heartily concur in the principles enunciated by the meeting. Yet properly to estimate the degree of importance attaching to this public display, it may be as well to observe that of the twenty thousand spectators present but a *minimum* thought it worth their while to join the Protestant societies there represented. In the eyes of the people these societies have one great shortcoming. They are distinct enough in what they repudiate, being implacable in their antagonism to the dogmatic views advocated by the Protestant and other Christian Churches; but they are less definite in what they affirm. Indeed, beyond recommending the lofty moral principles inherent in Christianity, they leave their members very much to find out for themselves what to believe and what to reject on the great questions of Providence, prayer, immortality, &c. The reason of this singular reticence is probably a wish not to deter any latitudinarians from joining however different their opinions may be on the all-important topics just alluded to; but, instead of effecting this comprehensive object, they have missed their aim entirely. It seems that a creed which does not shock some, lacks the power to attract others. What the people really want is not an outcry against the Pope, but to have their own religious doubts set at rest by some powerful mind, pious and at the same time enlightened. Educated men may not even require this, at least not consciously, being either too indifferent on the subject, or else devising some novel system for themselves; but the masses are yearning for some one to restore the faith they have lost, or to teach a new, and to them more acceptable, form of belief.

BERLIN, *June* 2, 1869.

CHAPTER IV.

AN ASSASSIN IN THE BERLIN CATHEDRAL.

"I BELIEVE in God the Father, God the Son, and God the Holy Ghost."

"You lie!"

A shot, a cry, general commotion.

On Sunday, August 8, in the presence of a numerous congregation, this sacrilegious scene was enacted in the Cathedral Church of Berlin. The Rev. H. Heinrici was standing before the altar, reciting the Belief, when a young man, rising from a front seat and interrupting the clergyman, gave him the lie, and at once discharged a pistol at his breast. The next moment he was in the hands of the sexton, and quietly suffered himself to be led away to the vestry. A portion of the congregation, seated at a distance, having heard the report and seen the curling smoke, without any definite notion of what was going on, immediately began to move towards the door, and created considerable tumult; but those near the altar, who had been witnesses of the daring attempt, retained their seats. In preserving their composure they but imitated the noble example of the clergyman whose life had just been placed in such jeopardy. The Rev. H. Heinrici was unhurt; nor had the moral firmness of the man whose body the ball had missed been shaken. No sooner had the trying interlude, the details of which seem to have been observed with terrible distinctness by those near, come to an end than the intended victim calmly resumed reading the Creed, and with redoubled fervour proclaimed that Belief the utterance of which had imperilled his life. After this the service was continued in accordance with the prescribed ritual. The Rev. H. Heinrici left the altar, when the Rev. Dr. Kögel ascended the pulpit and preached a sermon, in which he introduced a passage expressive of his thanks to God for the miraculous escape of his clerical brother. Quiet had been speedily restored, and the greater portion of the congregation, agitated as they were by the most powerful emotions, left the church only after the final benediction.

In the meantime the criminal had been conducted by a policeman to the nearest station, and examined by a superior officer. To all the questions put to him he replied with the utmost frankness and composure. He said:—

"My name is Biland. I am nineteen years of age, a Protestant, and the son of a blacksmith, in the village of Lank, county of Lower Barnim, a few miles from Berlin. My parents sent me to a grammar-school, wishing me to become a candidate for the ministry in the Established Church. But my eyes were soon opened to the falsehood of the creed I was expected some day to teach, and my dislike was increased to disgust when I perceived that many of those professing to believe it were liars at heart. I refused to pursue a career which had become so hateful to me, and resisted all attempts of my parents to force me to persevere. Eventually I saw myself left by them to my own devices, and began to study art— the dramatic art, I mean. I wished to become an actor and to preach to the public in my own way; but the religious mendacity rampant around me gave me no rest. Some I saw uttering deliberate untruths, while others, knowing them to be such, listened with contemptuous indifference. Gradually I taught myself that some striking deed was indispensable to rouse the public mind from its apathy and chase away the mists of superstition. I, therefore, determined to seize the first favourable opportunity that offered for shooting a clergyman while in the act of uttering his accursed perjuries. I have done it. I cast the ball myself and have done my best to render the shot fatal. I am sound in body and mind, and scorn the suggestion that I have acted under the disturbing influence of temporary insanity. I perfectly knew what I was about, and am convinced there are many able to comprehend the disinterestedness of my purpose, though they may, perhaps, not approve the method chosen to compass it. My design was to shoot Mr. Heinrici, and I was prepared to pay the penalty of the deed."

Such in substance was the statement of the reckless, misguided young man. Inquiries seem fully to confirm his words. His having missed at a distance of three paces at first gave rise to the surmise that he had fired with blank cartridge; but it is only too true that there was a ball in the barrel. The course of the ball has been exactly traced. Passing within an inch of the clergyman's head, it penetrated the open balustrade of the gallery, in which the *Dom Chor*— celebrated for its vocal performances—was stationed, and grazed the cheek of one of the choristers, a boy of twelve. The little fellow, although his cheek instantly began to swell, did not leave the church, but sang his allotted part to the end. The Prince Admiral Adalbert, the only member of the Royal family present, when the service was over, hastened to express his sympathy to the two clergymen and the little chorister boy.

The event throws a light upon the sad state of religion in this country. I am afraid the prisoner was right in supposing that many will appreciate his motive, though they will abhor the deed. I have previously stated in these columns that the majority of educated men in Germany are estranged from the dogmatic teaching of the Christian creed—estranged from it to the extent of disbelieving the sincerity of many of the clergy. Only a small fraction of the nation attends Divine service; of the educated, more especially, those met with in church on a Sunday are few and far between. To give you a characteristic instance: A few days ago, in a famous watering-place, I was in a church listening to a clergyman lamenting the frivolity of those who hoped to be benefited by the medicinal waters, and yet neglected to attend Divine service and pray for a blessing. The intention of the censorious preacher was certainly a praiseworthy one; the more the pity that so few were there to profit by it. Out of the 1,800 visitors recorded in the *Kurliste*, but five men and twenty of the gentler sex had cared to come, the rest of the congregation consisting of natives.

It is true there is a sprinkling of believers left in every part of the country, and there are whole districts in which Protestant or Catholic orthodoxy may be said to prevail to this day. But these are exceptions —*rari nantes in gurgite vasto*. The Wupperthal, on the borders of Westphalia, is a tower of Lutheranism; the adjoining Münsterland is more Catholic than Rome itself; but who expects belief on the gay Rhine or in latitudinarian Brunswick, although situate in such close propinquity to these stricter localities? To take a broader view, who that knows modern Germany will call it a Christian land, either in the sense Rome gives to the term, or in the meaning Luther attached to it? Roman Catholicism mainly exists among women and in the lower classes; and the Augsburg Confession, to maintain which Germany in the Thirty Years' War suffered herself to be cut to pieces by Austria and Austria's allies, has long ceased to be the authority it was, and, instead of the adamantine foundation of public belief, is now-a-days a mere ornamental decoration appended to the intellectual *status* of the land. In whatever section of society you may happen to move, there is the undeniable fact that the dogmatism of St. Athanasius and the statutes of the Council of Nice have entirely ceased to be a living power. Scholars have begun to denominate Christianity an Asiatic religion, and the public, proud of their vaunted European enlightenment, accept the degrading name.

And yet there is nothing like a religious movement going on in the country. Though Christianity is denied, no pains are taken to prove the why or wherefore. Latitudinarian sects are sometimes attempted to be formed, but soon abandoned and consigned to oblivion as idle and superfluous. The truth is that the majority of the educated, in their insidious march towards Rationalism, have advanced beyond acknowledging the necessity of any creed. Not content with rejecting the Bible, whose dogmas they regard as entirely exploded by the moral, historical, and scientific criticisms of the day, they have begun to doubt whether any teaching on transcendental subjects can be required to promote virtue. Most, indeed, profess to believe in God and immortality; but if you examine their opinions more closely, you will easily discover they have but confused notions on the relations between the Creator and mankind, and even deny or ignore the duty of aspiring to a more definite knowledge on the subject. Others, more daring in their conclusions, or coarser in their feelings, go the length of questioning the possibility of God's interfering with the self-supporting machinery of the world, look upon prayer as a Pagan rite, and sometimes become so irrational as to consider the very existence of a God as problematical. By the side of these cultivated infidels the masses vegetate in traditional attachment to the forms of Christianity without any warm interest for or against the dogma. To crown all, the Government force the children of all parties alike to learn the *Catechism* by heart, and in proportion to the spread of infidelity are intent upon cramming the youthful mind with texts and hymns. Yet the scriptural antidote is so unavailing to stem the progress of the tide that people do not even think it worth their while to remonstrate against it. In the present intellectual atmosphere of the country they are pretty certain that a boy of fifteen disbelieves the texts he has been compelled to learn at ten. There is a strong and growing impression, that the Christian creed has become too obsolete for anyone to take the trouble of warring against it. Men smile at the vain endeavours of the Protestant Governments of the country to inculcate orthodoxy, and are rather amused than otherwise by the zeal of the Catholic priesthood to establish convents in Lutheran localities—nay, in Berlin itself. They will not condescend so much as to form an estimate of the mental condition of a Popish priest; while as to the Reformed clergy, they regard some as enthusiasts, others as hypocrites, and the rest as unreflecting dunces; all equally destined to die out in a couple of generations. In this latter expectation they are confirmed by the fact that, although the majority of those embracing the ministry have recently, from sheer terror of the growth of Atheism, begun to be severe dogmatists, there is not always the requisite number coming forward to fill up vacancies. Even the sons of the lower classes, who in these days of decay in the Church supply a very large portion of its beneficed members, are not always numerously enough attracted by college stipends and lenient examinations to satisfy the demand. To many of the laity, therefore, Biland's deed will appear an insane attempt to effect what, in the natural course of things, will come of itself.

It cannot, however, with fairness be asserted that this lamentable state of things has rendered the Germans less moral than other more orthodox nations.

The excellence of the Christian moral doctrine remains unimpugned. Though the fear of condign punishment in the world to come has sensibly diminished, a sort of æsthetic recognition of the beauty of the Good among the educated aids in inculcating the appreciation of Duty. In the lower strata of society the simplicity and openness of the national character, together with the universality of elementary instruction, contribute to make the lack of more exalted motives of action less sensibly felt. Honour and honesty are as much respected as ever, and the criminal statistics continue to give favourable evidence of the condition of public morals. The rabble of the large cities, however, a class which from its nature is not very apt to succumb to æsthetic qualms, or to obey the behests of decency under the present dispensation, has become uncommonly coarse, unscrupulous, and blackguardly. Prussia has fewer crimes to chronicle than England, but the Berlin rate of illegal sin is comparatively higher than that of London.

It remains for me to add a line concerning a class, numerically small, but to which an important part will be, perhaps, allotted in the needful work of paving the way for the removal of the existing spiritual anarchy. A small fraction of cultivated minds view with sorrow the absence of definite religious convictions in the people. This minority—a scattered flock, who feel in unison, but have not as yet sufficiently developed their principles to proceed to action—endorse the notions of the majority respecting the alleged inadequacy of the ancient creeds; but they are persuaded that human reason suffices to establish those religious axioms they suppose to be required for the safe guidance of our career on earth. They consider it a grave duty to make this loftiest use of our reasoning faculties, and see no happiness for mankind unless this primary obligation be satisfied. They believe in God, hope for immortality, and, though contending that no revelation is or ever was required, to render man pious and good this side of the grave, yet readily acknowledge their inability to form an adequate estimate of our condition in a future state. It appears, however, that the men, who may be numbered among this class, are not agreed on the vital questions of personal responsibility and the power of prayer. They seem to anticipate that the solution of these alleged problems will give the signal for a new religious era and the foundation of the Germanic Church of the future. Pending this desired consummation, the earnestness of their reverential feelings, manifested in many scholarly and popular books, has had this beneficial influence on the general tone of the public mind, that Christ, though no longer regarded as a person in the Trinity, is recognized universally as the most sublime moral phenomenon in the history of mankind. As a rule, I believe, those advocating these opinions may be set down as members or, to a certain extent, friends of the Protestant Association, of which more anon.

BERLIN, *August* 11, 1869.

CHAPTER V.

THE PRUSSIAN CLERGY.

No more characteristic symptom of the prevailing indifference to anything connected with religion could be adduced than the absence of any excitement in consequence of young Biland's attempt to shoot a clergyman for repeating the Creed. In most papers the event is treated as any other common-place crime would be. A brief report, a few additional facts the day after, and the matter is dismissed. What besides has been printed on that terrible incident limits itself to a few lines in a couple of papers. One Conservative journal improves the occasion to charge the latitudinarian majority of the people with the preposterous design of outlawing their pastors; another denounces the constitutional propensities of the times as the real cause of murder, disbelief, and every other description of wickedness. The Liberal organs preserve an all but absolute silence. The more moderate, while they have no wish to uphold the Creed, yet feel a certain delicacy in attacking it at the moment of one of its professors being shot at; the coarser and more extreme ones are partly gagged by the fear of the public prosecutor, and partly look upon the occurrence as too miserably insignificant to deserve a leader. Being religious, or rather irreligious, in its origin, it in their eyes belongs to the category of obsolete antiquities, concerning which it does not become a rational being to waste a word. All that has been elicited from this portion of the Press is a significant anecdote indicative of their contempt of the clergy as well as of those who think it worth their while to annihilate them. A butcher, they tell you, a genuine Berliner, who had not for many years seen the inside of a church, happened to be in the Cathedral on the Sunday of the attempt. The reason for his appearance was to show the building to a friend from the country. As he was at some distance from the altar he heard the report of the pistol, but did not see who fired it. Amazed at this strange accompaniment to the Liturgy, he exclaimed, "That's a new dodge, I declare. When I was a boy they never fired guns when the Creed was said." The point of the anecdote is the representing the man as having had time to forget the arrangements of the service so utterly as to be capable of conceiving the monstrosity of pistol accompaniment as possible. A pretty joke, is it not?

To a certain extent the antipathy to the Church, which comes out in this story, is induced by the attitude of the clergy itself. After vainly endeavouring for some eighty years to come to an understanding with the progressive latitudinarianism of the age, the Protestant clergymen of Germany have at last become very orthodox. Upon the political movement of 1848 extending to religion, and imparting a daring determination to those rationalistic tendencies which had long been entertained in a feebler degree, the clergy perceived that, unless they were prepared to surrender unconditionally, nothing remained for them but steadfast resistance. Then the majority turned with new fervour to the ancient faith, and, by this unanimous move, have since exercised a powerful influence upon the opinions of young candidates for office; the rationalistic pastors who remain are few, and are nearly all men well stricken in years. This general change in the clergy did not, however, at first become very perceptible to the public. As formerly, most of the working rectors and curates were satisfied with ascending the pulpit once a week, and rating their congregations soundly, taking good care on week-days to comport themselves like ordinary mortals, and give no offence to individual members. Their reserve was facilitated by a German Protestant pastor not being expected to visit his parishioners, and advise them in their social and spiritual needs. In this country an Evangelical minister preaches, christens, marries, and buries, remaining all the while as utter a stranger to his flock as any other government functionary whose intercourse with the public is limited to business transactions in his office. But recently a portion of the orthodox clergy—a portion numerically small, though for its activity and achievements important—has distinguished itself by a more decided deportment. It consists of the zealous, who deem it a sacred duty to avow themselves at such a wicked time as the present, and manfully fight against the cancer of disbelief; of the vehement, who have a constitutional aptitude for scolding and threatening; and of sundry others, who may be described as disciplinarians, intent upon asserting their position, even should they be compelled to call in the aid of the secular power. In their sermons all three categories oppose the spirit of the age with an unrelenting harshness that confirms outsiders in their favourite axiom of the incorrigibility of the Church. They have gone the length of condemning the whole science of the century. They have denounced as so many heretics Goethe, Schiller, and all the other leading classics, at once the pride and the flower of the nation. One of them has recently scandalised Berlin by asserting that the earth does not turn round the sun, and calling the opposite notions of a colleague a sign of disbelief; another considers philosophy a dangerous kind of nonsense; a third accuses the Press generally of leading people on to perdition. What they all recommend as the only means to save the erring souls of the community is that very belief in miracles which public opinion rejects as fable. In a people so mentally obstinate as the Germans the antagonism of the opposing parties is thus whetted until reconciliation seems impossible. Already things have gone so far that men who have had a University education scarcely dare go to church lest they be taken for hypocrites or sentimental enthusiasts.

An even more marked impression than by their sermons has been produced by the acts of some of these members of the *ecclesia militans*. In Mecklenburg, where the ancient forms of orthodoxy prevail, the clergy insist upon supplementing baptism by a ceremony intended to exorcise the devil. The other day a landed proprietor, having been blessed with an addition to his family, petitioned the Grand Duke, in his capacity of *Summus Episcopus*, to be released from this antiquated rite. But no answer being vouchsafed, the exorcisms were duly administered. In the Prussian Established Church no regard is had in christening to the alleged ability of the Evil One to convey himself into the bodies of infants; yet conflicts will sometimes occur even there—conflicts which, though they are in reality called forth by the conscientious scruples of the clergy, still strike the public as studied impertinences. In Novaves, a village near Potsdam, a weaver a fortnight ago presented his child for baptism. The clergyman refused to perform the ceremony unless the father at once repeated the Creed. He had, he added, special reasons for doubting the soundness of the father's belief, and would not admit the infant within the pale of Christianity to be afterwards brought up by a heretic. To this the weaver replied that, as he was a rational being, he could not be expected to recite the Creed; in return the clergyman threatened that if the weaver did not submit he would sue the proper Court for an order that the child, as it had been born in the bosom of the Protestant Church, should be also brought up by real Protestants. In other words, he threatened to move for a decree that the child should be taken from its father and handed over for education to an orthodox guardian.

What was the weaver to do? Were he to accept the challenge and go to law the case might be decided against him, as the statutes do not seem to be very lucid on this head. On the one hand, there is the plain legal obligation of every Prussian to have his infants received into some religious community. On the other hand, it does not seem to be quite certain whether a father belonging to the Established Church is entitled to have his child recorded in the registers of another denomination as long as he himself is really or nominally a Protestant. To extricate himself from this dilemma in a way consistent with his views, the objectionable parent had no other means than to join a Free Congregation—a sort of religious, or rather irreligious, sect, whose peculiarity it is to acknowledge no Creed whatsoever. Accordingly he left the Church, embraced the new disbelief, and thus secured for himself the right to have his child likewise enrolled in that body. The story got into the papers, and even the most moderate organs of the public press spoke with indignation of the "intolerant priest." That, from the ecclesiastical point of view, the clergyman might, perhaps, have conscientiously doubted whether he was entitled to leave a Christian child in a heretic's hands, nobody will for a moment admit. In the present aspect of religion the public simply deny the right of any clergyman, in his actual official intercourse with his parishioners, to carry out the commands and prohibitions of that Creed which they permit him to emphasize as much as he likes while theorizing in the pulpit. Nor can it be denied that their reasonings are supported, and their claims encouraged by the accommodating spirit evinced by the clergy as a whole. A few hotspurs excepted, the whole host of the clergy have not the remotest idea of imitating their brother of Novaves, and preferring a demand which could not become general without leading to serious consequences.

A more sensational story still occurred in Berlin not so long ago. A bridal couple were standing before the altar to be married. Unfortunately for them, the officiating clergyman had heard that the young people would in a few weeks have again to request his services at the baptismal font. In the speech with which, according to custom, he opened the ceremony he allowed himself to allude to the prospective event. Then, becoming heated with his theme, he took upon himself to enact the representative of an avenging Deity, reprimanded the weeping bride, and wound up by boxing her ears. Against this terrible affront the bridegroom remonstrated with wonderful meekness.

His one object being to be married, and by marriage to repair the past, he said only a few exculpatory words to the vituperative priest, and requested him to proceed. Amid the tears of the ladies and the rage of the gentlemen present the rite was accomplished. On arriving at home the bride became ill and the following day was delivered of a dead child. The thing got wind and was discussed in the public press, though, of course, those immediately concerned would have preferred to keep it a secret. Upon this, the pugilistic clergyman at once wrote to a Conservative paper, declaring the whole story a lie, and not even condescending to explain how it was that such an extraordinary invention could have been fabricated at his expense. At this juncture the young husband, a music master, finding concealment out of the question, resolved upon having the only satisfaction possible, and brought an action against the self-alleged innocent. At the hearing of the case eleven persons took their oath that the blow had been given. Unheeding their depositions, the clergyman persisted in his denial, and, as his sole defence, referred the judges to the evidence of his own conscience and God's knowledge of his inward thoughts. The Court, in pursuance of the ordinary rules affecting the testimony of witnesses, left his conscience alone, and sentenced his body to three months' imprisonment. At the same time, the favour of "extenuating circumstances" being accorded him, he was allowed the option of either going to gaol or paying a fine of three hundred thalers. But no sentence of a mere earthly judge could shake *him*. He knew too well his own worth, appealed for a reversion of the sentence to a higher court, and in the meantime appeared again in the pulpit to justify himself before his congregation. The ecclesiastical authorities did not interfere. It had been generally expected they would have suspended him from office pending the final decision of the case; but no such decree was issued, and in this unsettled state the matter remains to this day. The Conservatives pretend to regard the accused as innocent; the Liberals assert that his being a strict believer is the cause of his statements being credited by the ecclesiastical authorities, who otherwise must have prohibited him from performing Divine service. All tongues are busy with the event, and many a heart is sore.

Were the majority of the public as unanimous in their views concerning some new and more eligible form of religion as they are in their objections to the doctrine and working of the present Church, we should not have to wait long for a radical reform. But there is the defect. Even those yearning for the establishment of some new mode of worship cannot agree upon a sufficient number of tenets to form a Church; whereas the masses are satisfied with a vague belief in God, and, though secretly longing for something more definite, are, while it seems unattainable, consoling themselves with the notion that any distinct form of religion is superfluous. It is on account of their objecting on principle to the existence of every Church that they do not care to leave the Establishment and create some new sect. There are, indeed, a number of rationalistic congregations in existence, but to join them is considered as equally affected as to attend the sermons of the orthodox clergy.

Thus the two hostile streams are flowing side by side in separate beds,—the stream of Rationalism, a still, but wide and deep expanse, threatening to swallow up the whole country; and the stream of Orthodox belief, a noisy, rushing torrent, intent upon fertilizing the fields, but by the vast lake of heresy confined to the irrigation of some remote nooks and ingles. What will the end be?

BERLIN, *August* 14, 1869.

CHAPTER VI.

A BERLIN CONVENT.

MOABIT is the north-western suburb of Berlin, famous for its Biblical name, its ironworks, and its beer. Its name, according to metropolitan tradition, was given it by French gardeners. Settling here after the repeal of the Edict of Nantes, and finding the sterility of the sandy soil a little too bad, the irascible Frenchmen are said to have bestowed upon their place of refuge the ungracious appellation *"terre maudite."* This occurring at a period when, as it would appear, the Berliners were better versed in the Bible than in the French grammar, the foreign term was misinterpreted, and supposed to refer to the wicked enemies of the Jews, the Moabites, whose patronymic became thus perpetuated in this northern capital. More noted than the misnomer are the ironworks of the locality. On that barren plain, in the course of time, were erected many enormous structures, devoted to industry, in which the manufacture of engines, porcelain, beer, &c., having been set on foot by intelligent capitalists, now employs some fifteen thousand workmen of superior skill and consequent success; and as wherever in this country artisans and beer abound music gardens are sure to spring up, Moabit has ended by becoming the El Dorado of landlords, and the paradise of the pleasure-seeking votaries of Terpsichore from the whole town.

This home of the genuine Berlin mechanic, with his roughness, his quickness, and irreverent wit, has now been chosen by the Catholic Church for the establishment of a monastery. A more uncongenial soil, one would imagine, it would be difficult to discover anywhere. But the *ecclesia militans*, we are triumphantly informed in its Berlin weekly,* having passed over from the defensive to the offensive, no longer hesitates to provoke public opinion in any part of the world. Just because Moabit is purely Protestant, and in no way ascetically inclined, the promoters of the Catholic interest selected it as the site of the first monastery that has existed in Brandenburg since the great clearing out at the Reformation. And not of one monastery alone, but of two. Having once resolved upon so striking a proceeding

* "Märkisches Kirchenblatt," the Catholic organ of this capital.

as the importation of the cowl to the biting latitude of Berlin, they thought to improve the occasion as much as possible, and made the sacred establishment a sort of "mother-house" for others yet to be formed. For the present the new convent has been occupied by Dominicans and Franciscans, one of which fraternities will remove whenever the means can be obtained for setting them up independently. Pending this both are to endeavour to draw other Orders after them to come to this province and exert themselves for its reconversion to the tenets of the Papacy. It is not to be wondered at that in the eyes of those who have bestowed time and money to bring about this notable result and pave the way, as they imagine, for something better, the return to Central Prussia of the religious anchorites should have been regarded as a great, nay, a truly historical event. So they determined upon marking it with due *éclat*. The four female orders (Ursulines, Elisabethans, Daughters of St. Borromeus, and Ladies of the Good Shepherd) which in the last twenty-five years have crept back to Berlin, entered this capital with such a studious absence of all outward demonstration that their very existence in our midst remains unknown to the majority of the natives to this day; but the monks took

A Berlin Convent.

care to advertise their arrival to the whole town. In their opinion, the day has evidently come when monks may avow themselves in the very heart of Protestantism, heedless of the criticisms of the impious or the taunts of a scurrilous press.

Accordingly, the new monastery was opened with a celebration accessible to the general public. This ceremony was performed on the 4th of August, and consisted in the consecration of the church appertaining to the bipartite convent. Of Dominicans and Franciscans only a small number were present; the more noticeable, therefore, was the crowd of spectators, devout and curious. A good many of the 30,000 Catholics scattered among the 800,000 inhabitants of Berlin turned out to attend; with them came not a few Protestants, bent upon seeing so unprecedented a sight. Mass having been performed, one Herr Müller delivered the speech of the day. Herr Müller is a gentleman of, it is said, priestly rank, who has been selected by the Bishop of Breslau to direct the business of the various Catholic societies at this capital. The better to qualify him for his task, he had the title of *Geistlicher Rath* conferred upon him by the Pope. Latterly he achieved notoriety by writing in the half mystic, half comical style peculiar to some gentlemen of his cloth, and of which honest Father de Santa Clara, of Vienna memory, will ever remain the unequalled prototype. Of his blunt eloquence the following extract from his inaugural address is a good specimen. Having first offered up a prayer, he said, among other things :—

"The Dominicans and Franciscans here meet in friendly co-operation. They do so here and now. It is necessary to emphasize the *here* and the *now*. They make their appearance in this capital of the Prussian State—nay, in this suburb of Moabit, famed for its sensuous indulgence of self. They open this place for religious exercise, at a moment when in another State, and that an essentially Catholic State, a fanatic storm has arisen against convents, when the very principle of monastic institutions is attacked in Austria, and a flood of hatred, rage, and calumny poured upon our defenceless heads. That at such a juncture as this we should be enabled to consecrate one, nay two, monasteries at Berlin, is an event the importance of which can only be surpassed by the fact that the religious orders to whom this new abode will be dedicated are not charitable, but purely contemplative orders, spending their whole time in prayer. In sensuous Moabit the Dominicans will henceforth be engaged in reflecting on the healing powers of the rosary, the Franciscans in meditating on the five wounds of Christ. As far back as Frederick the Great's reign Dominicans preached in a Berlin church. In permitting their second return, then, the Prussian Government have only imitated their former tolerance."

In reporting this speech, the Berlin papers thought it necessary to accompany it with commentaries, hereby deviating from their usual course of studied indifference to religious topics. A monastery at Moabit! To the Berlin ear it sounded pretty much the same as to the Londoner would the report that the Chinese Emperor had located a college in Cornhill for the spread of the official Mandarin philosophy in the British Isles. To adore the rosary and the "five wounds" in close vicinity to the sooty smithies, where the hammer and file are never at rest in the hands of industrious but, alas! too rationalistically inclined men,—it seemed to be a contrast almost too great to be believed. Town-talk turned upon it for a day or two, and the journals could not but advert to so startling a phenomenon. The occasion not being likely to inspire them with a deeper respect for religion than is ordinarily evinced by popular editors in this country, their remarks were conceived in a sarcastic, not to say a scoffing spirit, to illustrate which I will quote a few lines as a specimen. The *Volks Zeitung,* one of the most popular journals of Berlin, thus begins a leader on what it calls the miracle of Moabit :—

"Among the Moabites, close to sinful Berlin, a great miracle has been wrought. Thereat the Ammonites and the Jebusites, the Amorites and Canaanites will be amazed. The heathen will be in fear like a woman in travail. They will clap their hands and cry out, 'Come, let us go unto the new Jerusalem, whence issues the word of truth, for there the face of the earth has been revived.' There have united the sole dispensers of salvation, the sons of St. Dominicus and the sons of St. Franciscus. There they are, sitting snugly in their new and comfortable abode. The one set have nothing else to do than to tell their beads, while the others engage in profound meditation on the five wounds of Christ. And yet they are destined to wrestle with the giant of disbelief, who will not cease to ridicule Zebaoth and to abuse the children of the faith, that are to bring salvation to the world, and by their prayers to defend heaven itself against the fury of the raging Titans."

The close of this characteristic article is as follows :—

"The world is expected (by Mr. Müller) to look upon the foundation of this new monastery as an event of the highest importance. We, for our part, are convinced that the only emotion awakened among our compatriots will be that of satisfaction at the degree of culture which allows such scenes to be witnessed without public fanaticism being aroused against them."

This latter expectation has not been realised. After reading in their papers violent articles against the monastery for a couple of days, the Berliners, or, rather, the Moabites, assembled *en masse* in front of the monastery and began to throw stones. But for the timely interference of the police worse might have occurred than the smashing of the windows and the terror of the monks. The same scene was repeated on a subsequent evening. On one of these occasions a man is said to have harangued the masses, and told them that the notorious Tetzel, whose traffic in indulgences gave such an impetus to the Reformation, was a Dominican, which did not tend to allay the wrath of the multitude. However, the good Fathers were protected by the police, and, but for a shocking fright they had soon afterwards, would not have dreamt of evacuating their retreat. Sunday last, a trivial incident at Moabit led to one of those affrays between the police and the populace which may be considered as inseparable from metropolitan institutions, and certainly are among the most popular enjoyments of this city. Some juggler had advertised that he would ride a velocipede placed high on a rope. The blacksmiths and engineers of the industrious suburb, who from the nature of their profession take a keen interest in mechanical feats, crowded round the arena to gaze at this latest acrobatic wonder; but what was their disappointment when they perceived the velocipede to be tied to the rope in such a way as to render an accident impossible. Not humane enough to derive satisfaction from this cautious display of selfishness, they, on the contrary, considered themselves cheated of the awful emotion they thought they had a right to expect. Their resentment was increased by the juggler, as an additional attraction, calling himself a Swede, when, as appeared on his being examined by a travelled stoker, he was entirely innocent of the Scandinavian tongue. For this twofold fraud he, poor fellow, found himself presently handed over to Judge Lynch, and had to undergo a most instructive reprimand at the hands of that demonstrative personage. Eventually the police tore him from the grasp of his castigators, which, however, could not be effected without their charging the crowd. Then began the ordinary heroic combat between Greeks and Trojans. The constables first had recourse to their clubs, then drew their swords, yet could not vanquish their adversaries. A shower of bricks eventually drove the guardians of the public peace from the field, when a detachment of cavalry was despatched, and soon routed the victors. A number of wounded, among them one with his right hand cut off, will have occasion to remember this Sunday's campaign with very mixed sensations. This row, which happened close to the monastery, gave the Fathers such a dose of Berlin pugnacity that they resolved to evacuate their newly-acquired asylum, and not return until a high wall has been built round the sacred precincts.

The opening of a convent at Moabit is but the crowning incident in a series of similar events witnessed here in the last twenty years. It is an interesting fact, that the revival of Protestant orthodoxy has been accompanied by a corresponding move on the part of the Catholic clergy. Catholicism, twenty years ago in a state of even greater decline than the Reformed faith, has profited by the ecclesiastical resuscitation of the latter, to undertake a similar campaign against the prevailing spirit of the age. What it lacks in vital power, it makes up for by the courage and energy of its fiery advocates. Within the period mentioned some hundreds of new monasteries are asserted to have been added to those previously existing in the various provinces forming modern Prussia. The number of nuns and monks in each does not seem to be great, nor can the expense incurred by their humble inmates—the greater part belonging to the lower classes—be very considerable. The Jesuits, too, have rapidly increased, and now muster in Germany over two thousand—a higher figure than any country, except France, can boast. Besides this augmentation of what may be called the official staff, religious societies have been formed of artisans and children, whose members being divided into different classes, each lording it over the other, have both piety and vanity gratified by joining these auxiliary clubs. Yet, from all the seed sown, little fruit is to be remarked, even among Catholics. Upon the whole, the religious feeling of Romanists in this country differs but little from that of Protestants. Shrines, indeed, may be multiplied and find devotees, who worship with real ardour, or sometimes with self-complacent sentimentality; but for all this the intellectual movement of the day progresses unimpeded, the colour of men's thoughts remains unmodified, and even those attending church and acknowledging the sanctity of the priesthood are in their views on worldly things not as visibly influenced as they ought to be, had they sufficiently realised the difference between their creed and nineteenth-century opinions. A most noticeable result this, when it is considered that every third man in Prussia is a Catholic. As to Protestants being attracted to Catholicism by the exertions of the priesthood, such a thing is almost unknown.

Herr Ernest de Bunsen does me the honour of animadverting upon two several items occurring in one of my recent letters on the state of religion in this country.* One objection is openly expressed, the other implied. As regards the first, he thinks the Germans may deserve the name of Christians, though they have ceased to be so in the sense Luther attached to it. But Herr de Bunsen has misconceived my meaning when he believes my remarks to have been occasioned by the German Protestants—the small sect of Old Lutherans excepted—now-a-days rejecting the particular tenets on which Luther differed from other Reformers. I trust it will appear from the whole

* Herr de Bunsen's letter is reprinted in the Appendix.

contents of my letter that in the passage referred to, as in the rest, I look upon Luther as the representative of Protestantism generally, and that in asserting the majority of the Germans to have ceased to be Protestants in Luther's sense, I meant to say they had ceased to be so in the sense attached to the term in the sixteenth century by any Protestant creed whatsoever. Whether I am right or wrong in this statement is another question. Herr de Bunsen, in his second objection, seems to decide against me. As it would require an essay to adduce the arguments which might be alleged to prove my case, I think I may content myself with saying that nearly *all* German writers who have latterly written upon the subject have more or less distinctly expressed the same opinion as myself. On this one point orthodox professors are agreed with moderate Latitudinarians and radical Rationalists; on this one point there exists concurrence between Professor Hengstenberg, of Berlin, Professor Schenkel, of Heidelberg, and Dr. Uhlich, of Magdeburg; on this one point we read the same verdict in the orthodox *Evangelische Zeitung*, the mediating *Breslauer*, *National* and *Protestantische Zeitung*, and the avowedly anti-dogmatical *Volks Zeitung*. They all either complain or rejoice, according to their respective views, that the Protestant dogmas are no longer recognised by the majority, especially not by the educated classes. It is satisfactory to perceive that most of them are also forced to admit that the spirit of Christianity at least survives. As regards Herr de Bunsen's not expecting enlightenment from me, on the important question as to what the dogmas of the Bible are, I can only observe that in writing my letter my intention obviously was not to solve religious problems, but to report on the state of public opinion respecting them.

BERLIN, *August* 18, 1869.

CHAPTER VII.

THE GERMAN PROTESTANT ASSOCIATION.

To oppose the action of the orthodox clergy and at the same time revive the interest of the latitudinarian laity in the affairs of Church and School, a special society was established a few years ago. Being the only attempt of the kind in the present phase of German scepticism, and deriving considerable authority from the many eminent and highly respectable names among its members, this association may be regarded as a feature in the history of the times. The members of this remarkable body have been recruited from those who, while they reject the inspiration of the Bible, yet differ from the vulgar rationalism of the day in this, that they acknowledge the duty of professing some modern form of religion, based upon the moral teachings of what they regard as a venerable, but, in many respects, obsolete book. The society has never very accurately defined the doctrine it intends to place in the stead of the ancient creed, but seems to prefer indefinite language when speaking on this point, and sometimes even alludes to the desired reform as an event not to be consummated just now, but which must be looked for in the future. All it has expressed a positive opinion upon, and enjoins on its members, is the duty of promoting the universal acknowledgment of Christian morality (*Christlich sittliche Lebensgemeinschaft*).

This body, which calls itself the German Protestant Association, was set on foot by a knot of well-meaning and temperate men belonging to the higher strata of the middle classes. At its head are distinguished professors of theology, and many other men of wealth, rank, and erudition, who justly enjoy the respect of their compatriots. Their principal way of appealing to the public is by holding annual meetings—each year in a different place—in which the proceedings of the ecclesiastical authorities are measured by a more or less rationalistic standard, and condemned accordingly. Speeches are also delivered on such occasions on the history of religion and similar subjects, intended to propagate the views of the society. For these annual meetings the members assemble from all parts of Germany, local meetings being sometimes, though rarely, held by those residing in the same town. Though all these assemblies are, as a rule, well attended by the members, they yet derive the greater part of their *éclat* from outsiders. A few of the larger towns excepted, there is not a place in which the members are sufficiently numerous to make an imposing show, or to satisfy their natural wish for notoriety and influence without calling in the general public. Invitations accordingly are always sedulously circulated in advance, and cordially responded to. There are plenty of people in nearly every part of this populous and intellectually inclined country who though they do not care to join a society whose professed object is opposition to orthodoxy, yet take intense delight in hearing orthodox views and proceedings strongly criticized once or twice a year. As to enrolling themselves in the lists of the society, the majority of latitudinarians do not see the use of it, notwithstanding the many and urgent appeals addressed them. The cause of their reserve is twofold. In the first place, as I have had occasion to remark in a previous letter, people believe the ancient faith to be utterly exploded, and only smile at what they regard as the vain endeavour of the Government to inculcate it afresh by preachers and teachers. Why, then, need they subscribe to a society making superfluous protests against what is no longer a living reality? On the other hand, they cannot understand what advantage there is in proclaiming the excellence of the code of Christian morals, never impugned even by advanced rationalists. To the million, therefore, the society, both in what it affirms as in what it denies, seems to have undertaken a work of supererogation.

The question whether the society is useful or the reverse has recently occasioned a controversy well calculated to illustrate its position and the general state of religion in Germany. I purpose extracting some articles and letters published in the course of this literary feud, accompanying them with such remarks as may be required for the better appreciation of their local features. For some time past the *Magdeburger Zeitung*, a paper of moderate views in politics and religion, has been pleading the cause of the society. To induce the educated classes to shake off their apathy, and energetically support a body which has so often petitioned for their help, that paper addressed them as follows:—

"The defects in the state of our ecclesiastical affairs can be only accounted for by the indifference of the cultivated classes. It is they who must be charged with the guilt of the present state of things. They have long turned the cold shoulder to all that concerns the Church. The scholar, the doctor, the artist, the merchant, the manufacturer, are content to devote themselves to their respective pursuits, and if in addition to their private interests they manifest any zeal beyond their immediate call in life, it is confined to politics. As to what occurs in the Church, they will not condescend so much as to notice it, and it is only when some narrow-minded parson denies the rotation of the earth that they are frightened or amused by the amazing stupidity of those theologians clinging to the letter of the law. Still it is this very set of theologians that directs the education of the humbler classes, and even exercises some influence upon the schools in which the children of well-to-do people are brought up. These religious fanatics have been long and assiduously engaged in opening a gap between Christianity and common sense, and converting our religion into a superstition and our thinking men into infidels. Is not this important enough to be looked after? Is it possible that our public and private life can be healthy if obliged to put up with such a Church? It cannot be so. The disease of the Church has begun to exercise a baneful effect on the people, driving them either into the arms of a coarse materialism, or else causing them to be enveloped in a mental obscuration very much resembling the normal condition of the pious Catholic. All this being undeniable, it is time we should remember our duty, and, were it only for the sake of the people and elementary instruction, take an earnest and abiding interest in the reform of our Protestant Church."

I have not heard of any marked impression being produced by these entreaties. The influence of orthodox preachers and teachers is simply ridiculed, and few can be brought to believe that the notions these antiquated ignoramuses—for such they hold them—try to instil need any antidote, except the spirit of this modern age, as administered in every newspaper paragraph, nay, in the conversation of all ranks. Such being the case, we need not be astonished that the moderate *Magdeburger Zeitung* should have received a sarcastic reply from a more radically-inclined journal. It was the Berlin *Volks Zeitung* which took upon itself to answer its gentler contemporary, and as I think that in this particular question the more advanced view is the one patronized by the cultivated classes as a whole, I will adduce the following from this Radical and popular organ of the capital :—

"We doubt that the complaints of the *Magdeburger Zeitung* will swell the numbers of the Protestanten-Verein. For that society to become popular it ought to go much farther. The enlightened theologians presiding over its councils evidently wish to effect a compromise between common sense and certain cardinal notions inherent in the old creeds. But common sense—lay common sense we mean—laughs at their artificial tonings down and smoothings over, and does not at all approve the attempt to reconcile the irreconcilable, made in the books of a Schenkel and his associates. The whole intellectual horizon of the period in which the myths and fables of religion were formed, is not only a matter of perfect indifference, but also something absolutely unintelligible to the men of this day. By the nineteenth century laity no interest is felt in watching the twistings and turnings of texts, practised by the more liberal-minded theologians in their desperate endeavour to find an atom of truth in these exploded legends. If it has been proved that the sky is not exactly the cupola, arching over the earth, which our ancestors supposed it, but only thin air, it cannot possibly concern us in what way theologians manage to account for the Ascension. Again, the interpretations devised as a means of explaining away what is objectionable in the notion of a Trinity, without absolutely relinquishing it, are far too cunning to gain the applause of those who do not see the good of dressing up fables to save appearances, when the substance has slipped away. That kind of theology which the leaders of the Protestant Association still cling to may be a respectable attempt of theologians to free themselves from the fetters of antiquated notions without directly adopting the views of this modern age; but the layman, who has no need to stick to tradition, regards this theological manœuvre as likely to produce clever excuses, but not wholesome truth. The layman sees the world as it is, and will not allow himself to be carried away by the artificial devices of the Protestanten-Verein."

Surely, if such be the suggestions of German common sense, there is no fear of its being worked upon by clerical means. For any danger, threatening them from this quarter, people have, then, no reason to combine. To protect himself against this feeble enemy every one gifted with common sense *à la mode* may, it is evident, be trusted to himself. As to the other ground of popular indifference to the Protestanten-Verein alleged by the *Volks Zeitung*,—viz., that it does not go far enough in its rejection of the Biblical doctrine—this is a mistake. Though the distinguished professors in the society are, it is true, inclined to explain the miracles in a half-and-half way, neither altogether orthodox nor absolutely rationalistic, they, in their capacity of members, do not object to more extreme rationalistic views. On the contrary, they are ready to admit to the society any one impressed with the beauty of Christian morals, even though he considers the Bible as an old book and no more. Professor Schenkel of Heidelberg, one of the most learned German theologians, who may be called the father of the society, has hastened to correct this mistake of the *Volks Zeitung*, and to proclaim that the Protestanten-Verein, as such, has no wish to uphold the Bible or any of the ancient creeds based upon it. In a very candid letter to the editor of the *Volks Zeitung*, dated Heidelberg, July 31, 1869, he expresses himself as follows:—

"The Protestant Association as such has but little in common with theology. It approves no theological system whatever, and has expressly and unmistakably pronounced against the preponderance of theological dogmatism of every shade. The association does not at all regard it as its legitimate object to reconcile our traditional theology or any single dogma maintained by it with common sense. It cares as little for the crafty interpretation of myths and miracles. What it wants is not to revive theology, but to revive Christianity, and renovate the Protestant Church in the spirit of evangelical freedom, in harmony with the intellectual development of the age. This is not a theological but a moral and a social task, and one that cannot be completed in a couple of years or by a few individuals, but requires the co-operation of the whole nation. If it has not yet been completed by the Protestanten-Verein, no reproach attaches to any one. The theological views of the individual members of our society—for instance, my views—are not those of the society. The society is tolerant towards all tolerant towards others, and admits all not denying the spirit of evangelical freedom, and willing to co-operate in the practical renovation of the Church. No layman, therefore, who joins the society is made to adhere to traditional formulæ."

Passing from what the society does not to what it does, the Professor continues :—

"The Protestant Association looks upon Ultramontanism, hierarchy, orthodoxy, and the intolerance manifested by some of our Protestant churches, as dangerous evils. While five-sixths of the inhabitants remain under the influence of priest or parson, and are but very scantily supplied with instruction, as statistics prove, we ought to exert ourselves to promote the religious and moral amendment of the people. From a semi-official statement it appears that within the last thirty years hundreds of new convents have been established in Prussia; nearly all theological professorships in our Universities are occupied by men of the strictest orthodoxy; the ecclesiastical authorities direct the Church of the most powerful of the German States in a like spirit, and thousands of clergymen are sowing a seed which will bear fruit, though certainly not the fruit of liberty and enlightenment. Religion is not only a strong force in history, but also a personal want of every individual. To neglect it has always impaired the progress of culture. It is a pity that the men of progress should so much less know how to estimate its influence than the men advocating retrograde movements. What a blessing for our people would be a free and enlightened Protestant Church! For the furtherance of Protestant spiritual liberty it is that the Protestant Association exerts itself."

The above confirms what I have said as to the indistinct language employed by the society in speaking of its aims. The society, we are told, aspires to have a free and enlightened Protestant Church and Protestant spiritual liberty. Unfortunately, these are such wide and indefinite terms, that when we have them we are at a loss what to do with them. Is the free and enlightened Church to have a creed, or is the rejection of dogma announced by the Professor destructive of all creeds whatsoever? If the adoption of a new creed be compatible with the annihilation of the ancient dogma, what creed will be substituted? Or, if it be premature to ask so pregnant a question, would it not be practicable to give us a general idea of what we have to expect? What, for instance, are the notions likely to be entertained by the new Church on the all-important topics of Providence, sin, and prayer? Upon all these points silence is maintained by the Professor, though speaking in his letter in behalf of his religious reforming society. Nor are the utterances that have emanated on other occasions from the body in question much more elucidatory. The most tangible avowal of doctrine I remember to have met with occurs in the resolutions passed by the second general meeting at Neustadt in September, 1867, where it was said that the essence (*Schwerpunkt*) of Christianity was not in the ecclesiastical dogma, but in the acknowledgment of Christian morality.* But even this leaves us with the vital questions still unanswered. Could we think that the free and enlightened Church of the future is to look upon these questions with as much indifference as the more advanced Radicalism of the day does, there would of course be no cause for surprise at this reticence; but then why found any new Church at all? To teach mere morality no Church is required, nor will such teaching stop the spread of Atheism, respect for the virtue of this world being quite compatible with the most perfect indifference to the Deity. This obvious truth has, in the outspoken *Volks Zeitung*, been made the theme of an article in reply to the learned Professor, which deserves to be quoted:—

"Assuming the Protestanten-Verein to share the convictions of its founder, it professes to believe religion has been a source of culture. Time-honoured as it is, we deny the truth of this antiquated axiom, and for our part assert that, consciously or unconsciously, it is no longer admitted by the educated classes. The essence of the religion of all nations consists in a moral code, which lays down the fundamental rules of

* These resolutions were proposed by Professor Schenkel, and carried almost unanimously.

social life. These fundamental laws are nearly identical everywhere, the slight variations which occur being mainly chargeable to the difference in the degree of culture marking the several races and stages of social development. This oneness of the moral codes is the necessary consequence of those laws having been derived from observation of human nature. Human nature being the same everywhere, the laws based upon it must be equally so. But in those early days, when people were too ignorant to perceive the natural process by which the laws in question were evolved, myths, fictions, and miraculous stories arose respecting the manner in which the human race had those axioms disclosed to them. These tales and fictions respecting the origin of moral law, when they gradually expanded and became consolidated into definite mythological systems, formed the second portion of the religious creeds, the religion or faith, properly speaking. They differ very much from each other, according to the different intellectual attainments of those who invented them, and the historical events, nay, even the character of the landscape, which influenced their minds. All these tales are mere fictions. Their most favourite incidents are miracles, and though none of them ever happened, the slightest variation in their tenour has frequently sufficed to set nation against nation, and inspire both with a ruthless desire to exterminate each other. In the fearful wars thus kindled, the real essence of religion, the moral law, has been but too often disowned and trodden under foot. The contention about these religious fables is one of the most shocking features in the history of the world, and has prevented whole generations from enjoying the benefit they might otherwise have derived from the moral law. In those dreadful days the religious stories which every one believed, though unable to ascertain their accuracy, were considered as infallible truth, to maintain which reason and logic had to be ignored. It was only after the discovery of some of the great laws of nature that man began to realize the difference between reality and fiction. Since then the conviction has gained ground by degrees that to quarrel about the origin of religion is to fight about fables, and that religion in reality consists only of that moral code the practice of which has never given rise to discord, nor ever will. Such being the case, and the world having at length realized the fact that, though knowledge and culture have influenced religion, they, in their turn, have never been advanced by her, it is only natural that our eyes should be opened to some other wholesome truths. At present, all civilized nations are aware that, wherever that class of society which makes a profession of contending about fables was armed with power over secular affairs, the decline of culture and the growth of evil were the inevitable consequences; at present, we are all endeavouring to prevent the said class of quarrelers about nothing from regaining their former sway over the destinies of mankind. To assert and act up to these principles is true liberty of conscience. Liberty of conscience, in the modern acceptation of the term, makes us perfectly indifferent as to what particular religion a man chooses to profess, provided he submit to the common code of human morality. If, in addition to acquitting himself of this supreme obligation, he takes delight in believing some fable or other, let him. If he feel tempted to assert that the moral code was originally proclaimed by Odin or Jupiter, Jehovah, Moses, or Jesus, it is all one to us, and we have not the slightest intention to dispute with him about it. We have outgrown that sort of controversy, and all we care for is that the State may remain as indifferent to it as ourselves, and not support any one of these legends by lending it the sanction of its authority."

Further on in the same article we read :—

"The Protestant Association is desirous to create a free and enlightened Protestant Church, from the establishment of which it expects great advantage to the nation. Praiseworthy as this object is, when compared to the attitude of our old orthodox established Churches, which are not at all free and enlightened, but, on the contrary, seek to coerce science and the convictions thereon based, still we doubt whether the Protestanten-Verein is in harmony with the spirit of our age, and the notions of the cultivated classes. Take them as a whole, those classes have no wish to form any new Church; nor would a new Church, were it Protestant, satisfy the requirements of the age. As to anticipating the progress of culture from the setting up of such a Church, it is quite out of the question. Culture is derived from knowledge, not from belief, however free and enlightened. The records of history teach that intellectual advancement made its greatest strides whenever and wherever the fetters of faith were taken off the human mind."

However audacious we may think these remarks, there is a logical sequence in them. Granting morality to be the one thing required, there is no further need of a Church. With the refinement moral teaching has gradually attained since the introduction of Christianity, no transcendental motives are required to make man ordinarily honest and kind. Whether this was always the case, whether the coarser morality of the past would have been sufficient without the aid of religion to work the same effect, is another question, which no one conversant with history will answer in the affirmative. Against this latter portion of the *Volks Zeitung* argument is directed a fresh letter with which Professor Schenkel has just closed the correspondence, and which I subjoin in full :—

"You ascribe to me the conviction that religion is the main source of culture. Assuming this to be my opinion, I cannot but qualify it by the remark that religion to me does not consist of myths, fables, dogmas, &c., but of those aspiring thoughts and feelings (*innere Ideenwelt*) by means of which the human soul becomes conscious of its relation to the Divine. From history I know that a new system of such aspiring thoughts and feelings has been disclosed to mankind by the Christian religion, although I am prepared to admit that the gift was presented in an inadequate and, in regard to this age, antiquated form. I concur with you in holding that to quarrel about this outward form is foolish, and may, in some cases, be a crime.

That the Protestant association approves my opinions on this head I have no doubt. Herein the *Volks Zeitung* and I are also of one mind. What we differ about seems to be this :—You maintain that no religion has ever been conducive to the advancement of culture; that all religions, as religions, are identical; and that all nations, irrespective of their religions, acknowledge the same moral fundamental laws for the regulation of social life. This history compels me to deny. It is a fact that two institutions of vital consequence in the annals of moral culture, slavery and polygamy, are at variance with the religious idea of Christianity, whereas they were considered as perfectly moral by civilized peoples before the advent of Christianity, and are to this day thus regarded by the Mahomedans. Christianity has a specific character, and the historical basis supplied by that character the Protestant Association acknowledges as its own. The Christian idea of the equality of all men in the sight of their Heavenly Father destroyed the assumption, so prejudicial to culture, that the right to keep slaves may be justly claimed by the privileged. Again, the Christian idea of the liberty of all men, and of the dignity of each individual as ennobled by Christ, did away with the prejudice that woman is a thing without rights, given man for his pleasure, and that children are no more than tools in the hands of their fathers. But even on the common ground of Christianity very different results have been worked out by different Churches, and very opposite influences have been exercised upon culture by the various religious communities. A Church, for instance, which enjoins the celibacy of the priest, recommends the indolence of monastic life, declares the mechanic repetition of certain forms of prayer as pleasing to God, and places between the Divine Being and the human conscience a mediator who pretends to have supernatural authority for his functions—such a Church must affect the moral culture of society in a way the reverse of what is wrought by a religious community which educates their clergy for family life, exalts industry and labour, strives to imbue daily life with a spirit of moral vigour, and allows the congregation the conduct of its own religious affairs. In this sense, and in this sense alone, I regard Christianity and Protestantism as sources of culture, and consider them none the less so because of religion having become before this, and being, perhaps, destined to become hereafter, a source of barbarism."

As the reader will observe, Professor Schenkel's objections are confined to the historical mistake the

Volks Zeitung commits in denying Christianity to have promoted the interests of culture. The fact that his adversary declares not alone against the Christian dogma, but against every description of faith, is passed over in silence by him. Nevertheless, it would no doubt be wronging the Professor and the Association in whose committee he plays such an important part were we to assume him to be on these vital questions at one with the Radical organ. His notions and those of the society do not exclude the necessity of a Church, and therefore must be assumed to include the necessity of having regard to the existence of a God—an inference corroborated by his speaking in the above letter (as, indeed, in many of his erudite works) of the Heavenly Father of mankind and the relation of the human soul to the Divine Being. Were the Protestant Association to advert to these topics oftener than they have hitherto done, and avow more definite notions on what they think the said relation between the soul and the Deity to be, they would probably acquire more decided weight with the people. According to the notions they might avow they would deter some and attract others, but, in any case, pave the way for a superior sort of authority to the one they now possess. With their present programme — the characteristic feature of which is reticence on so many important items—the Association offend the orthodox, appear superfluous to advanced latitudinarians, and do not even satisfy those who, looking upon the Bible as a human and fallible book, yet yearn for some guidance that shall enable them to obtain a certain belief respecting their position towards the Creator. If, notwithstanding that this is manifestly the case, a society established for the revival of religious life have so long kept from employing the most effective means for their purpose, and allowed the people they wish to rescue to sink more and more into dismal and dreary apathy, this must be regarded as another proof of the truth of the old experience, how difficult it is to effect a compromise between rationalism and religion.

The next meeting of the society will be held at Berlin on the 5th, 6th, and 7th of October. By a decree just published, the ecclesiastical authorities of the province of Brandenburg have denied the society the use of any church for this purpose, on the ground that "the society regards as justifiable even those interpretations of Biblical truth at variance with the cardinal doctrines of the Christian faith." This is the first instance of such rigour being observed towards them. The ecclesiastical edifices of the various minor

States, in which their annual meetings have been hitherto held, were always readily placed at the disposal of the society.

In reply to the letter of the Rev. C. H. H. Wright,* which appears in your impression of the 19th instant, nothing can have been further from my thoughts than to charge the German Protestant clergy with embracing orthodox views from a craven fear of the multitude. But it is probably not disrespectful to them to say that the length rationalism went has made many reject all idea of effecting an understanding with those modern philosophers they once regarded much more leniently. At any rate, this opinion seems to be permissible till such time as the Rev. C. H. H. Wright shall account in some other way for the marked conversion to orthodox tenets which began to occur among the German clergy in the reign of Frederick William IV.

BERLIN, *August* 24, 1869.

* Reprinted in the Appendix.

CHAPTER VIII.

THE BERLIN CONVENT.

SINCE adverting last to the subject, the monastery in the suburb of Moabit has been repeatedly assaulted by the mob. On one occasion the riotous multitude penetrated into the building, and the secular portion of the inmates had to defend themselves with hatchets and other weapons of civil warfare until rescued by the police. The shouts with which these attacks were accompanied left no doubt as to the cause of the irritation prevailing in Moabit. "How many have you already immured?" the besieging parties would cry out, tauntingly, with an unmistakable allusion to the terrible discovery lately made at Cracow. Others would ask the Father Superior, "how he dared charge the Moabites with the sin of sensuous enjoyment, when the worst they could be accused of was that they preferred beer to water, while his monks preferred alms to wages." As you may remember, reference to the beery propensities of the hard-working smiths of the locality had been made in Herr Müller's inaugural speech, and it is probable that this wanton provocation has done more to rouse bad feeling than anything else. However, the tumults, which at one time began to assume an ugly aspect, have at length been quelled by the energetic action of the constabulary, and there are no immediate apprehensions entertained as to the fate of the meditative Fathers. It appears that, frightened by the incessant hostilities, they left their ill-starred retreat for a few days, and returned only after a permanent garrison of thirty armed constables had been accorded them. This detachment of the public force still remains in the sacred edifice, and may be seen lounging about the cloisters and smoking irreverent cigars in precincts properly devoted to very different purposes. Apart from the merit or demerit attaching to monasteries, one cannot help thinking that if thirty officers are required for the protection of eight monks, the Protestant ratepayers of Berlin pay rather dearly for the whim of those of their Catholic townsmen who have thought fit to open such an exotic establishment at Moabit. At present church and monastery are under lock and key, and no visitors admitted. To remove all fear of further disturbance, a shooting match annually coming off at Moabit at this season, and attracting crowds of artisans, has been prohibited for this year. In addition to this precaution, the chief of the police—who in Berlin, as in most of the larger cities, is a nominee of the crown— has asked the Town Council to warn the inhabitants against damaging the convent, as all harm done must, according to law, be repaired by the municipality. Averse to admitting their liability before trial, the Town Council did not comply with this request, but there is no doubt that they will ultimately be obliged to pay. It is said that the damage done is estimated by the Fathers at three thousand thalers, and that above seventy persons have been arrested at the various outbreaks.

A noisy echo these rows had in a meeting held on Sunday last in a locality on the borders of Moabit. Educated men not thinking it worth their while to oppose anything so out of date as a monastery, the meeting was almost exclusively attended by operatives, and from the outset resembled the beginning of an *émeute* rather than a debate. Some of the speakers thought fit to represent monastic establishments as the chosen abodes of stupidity and vice. Others blamed the Government for tolerating convents, and yet raising difficulties about the free—*i.e.*, atheistic—congregations. Again, others asserted the Berliners deserved the disgrace of a convent in their city, having permitted their Protestant clergymen to teach doctrines scarcely distinguishable from Catholicism. If, these advocates of extreme measures contended, the Berliners were men, they would leave the Established Church in a body, thus exploding Protestantism and Catholicism, both, in point of fact, about equally bad. Thus the debate like a ball was tossed hither and thither, becoming more violent as more beer was drunk. Though the speakers and the audience were pretty well agreed, their fiery zeal gradually rose to such a height that the smallest sign of moderation was sufficient to cause an orator to be summarily ejected from the rostrum. The worst fate befel a Catholic, who ventured a few sentences in defence of the monks. For all reply he was dragged down, bonneted and kicked out of the assembly. In conclusion, two resolutions were passed. The one declares that "this meeting does not object to religion, but hates the abodes of vice and mental darkness yclept monasteries;" the other censures the Crown for entering in 1821 into an agreement with the Pope, in accordance with which the Catholic Church in this country is left free to administer its own affairs without the interference of the State. It was in consequence of this treaty—the resolution went on—that the monasteries abolished in 1810 were re-introduced into Prussia in 1821, and, if the Parliament knew what they were about, they would endeavour to repair this pernicious mistake, and turn out all monks and Jesuits. Thus with wordy explosions ended a meeting which the timid anticipated would lead to a renewal of the Moabit rows.

A peculiar attitude has during this mimicry of religious war been observed by the administrative and ecclesiastical authorities. In papers on excellent terms with the Government the inauguration of the monastery was at first spoken of with such marked benevolence that the public could not but conclude their rulers favoured the thing. According to the popular idea, this but too fully agreed with the orthodox principles pursued by the Minister of Ecclesiastical Affairs in the direction of the Protestant Church. In many parts of Northern Germany public opinion no longer very accurately distinguishes between Protestant and Catholic orthodoxy, and if a man be such a strict Lutheran as Herr von Mühler,* people think it a matter of course that he should patronise Catholicism also. But in this

* Herr von Mühler, the Secretary for Church and Education in the present cabinet.

particular instance their inferences were destined to meet with refutation. Scarcely had the indignation of the educated been aroused by that provoking speech at Moabit, scarcely had the artizans and mill-hands of the manufacturing suburb resorted to a telling method of resenting the taunt flung at them, than a paragraph appeared in some papers, stating on good authority that the chief of the metropolitan police had been entirely ignorant of the proposed establishment of a monastery. The Police President on such a question as this must be regarded as identical with the Minister of Internal Affairs, so that a disavowal referring to the one may be said to apply with equal force to the other. A like statement, but in an official form, was vouchsafed us by the Minister of Ecclesiastical Affairs, who says the first he heard of the monastery was that it had been opened. To render these revelations less startling to the public, who had always believed that no convent could be set up without a Government concession, a semi-official paper was instructed to announce that convents, being regarded as private societies, were not obliged to obtain a direct permit from the authorities. This, indeed, was an interesting disclosure. It implied that, in a country where it is difficult for any society to free itself from Government supervision, convents, though notoriously exercising considerable influence on those outside their walls, were looked upon as strictly private, and, consequently, exempt from every control. It implied, furthermore, that the Government had so long left the people under an erroneous impression on this important head, and that while every species of dissent was discountenanced, Catholicism had been practically favoured. Hence the feelings awakened by the Ministerial announcement were of a very mixed nature. People did not know whether they ought to rejoice that a liberal interpretation of the law had prevailed, at least, as regarded one description of societies, or whether they ought to be angry because of this exceptional liberalism having been confined to convents. They, moreover, thought they perceived a direct fostering of convents in the fact that as many of them as had asked for the right of acquiring property in their own name had been accorded this valuable privilege by the authorities. There is no doubt that the matter, which has long attracted the attention of the Liberal party, will, in consequence of these latest events, be discussed in the next Session of the Prussian Parliament. To a certain extent the Government will be able to defend themselves by pointing to the law of the land, which, protecting monks and nuns against all arbitrary dictates of their superiors, tends to loosen the cords of discipline, thus rendering convents less dangerous to inmates as well as to outsiders. Under several statutes enacted at different times, no monk or nun can be coerced into staying a moment longer in a convent than he or she chooses. To strengthen the protection afforded by these provisions, another law makes the Father Superior responsible for any punishment inflicted, even though it may have been borne with the hearty consent of the victim. Hence the imprisonment of a monk for a single hour within the walls of his convent, however willingly endured by the culprit, exposes the Superior to the same punishment that would be incurred by a private individual kidnapping and incarcerating another private individual for a like period. Equal strictness is observed with regard to blows and other personal injuries. If we add that no man is permitted to enter this state of bodily and intellectual bondage before his twenty-fifth, and no woman before her twenty-first year, it cannot be denied that the perils and hardships of monastic life are provided against as much as possible by the law. However, public opinion hates not only the more glaring deficiencies of convents, but the convents themselves, and, though certainly not much disquieted by their increase, yet views them as institutions which, if they could, would crush out intellectual life.

The leniency of the Prussian Government has certainly been turned to account by the priests. The first convent was re-established in 1821. In 1855 there were 69; in 1864 they had, by the revival of religious fervour in the priesthood, been increased to 243; by 1866 this figure had risen to 481, among them eight Jesuit Colleges. The number of monks and nuns, 960 in 1855, amounted to 5,259 in 1864, most of them being recruited from the humbler ranks of society. Not a few of the convents are situate in localities where the Catholics form only a *minimum* of the population. Even Eisleben, Luther's native town, has had one of these institutions bestowed upon it, because of a few Catholic mill hands and miners having been attracted there by the factories in the neighbourhood.

Now that the typhus epidemic has fortunately disappeared from the province of East Prussia, the Berlin Society for the relief of the sufferers has published a report, which may be recommended to the perusal of all interested in eleemosynary topics. The report draws a picture of ample and well-directed charity never equalled in Germany. When in the winter of 1868 famine and disease, the consequence of a failure of the crops and commercial stagnation, attacked the devoted province, the Berlin Society was formed by a number of influential residents, under the patronage of his Royal Highness the Crown Prince. In accordance with the principle laid down by their Royal Protector, the society gave alms only to the sick, providing work for the healthy, and, instead of money, paying them in provisions at a cheaper rate than they could have procured them themselves. The women were taught to spin flax; the men set to make roads and do other manual labour. By strictly adhering to this system, the society preserved the self-respect of the poor, diminished the cost of relief, and guarded against indiscriminate charity, so difficult to avoid at a period of a great national disaster. So prudent an application of their funds could not have been made without the active assistance of a number of local committees, endeavouring to ascertain the needs of every individual family, and relieve them accordingly, and the trouble these good men took in their benevolent work has certainly done as much to counteract the evils of destitution as the money itself. For the central direction of the various local committees, and the conduct of the society's business generally, the country is chiefly indebted to Herr George von Bunsen, who, as honorary secretary, had a praiseworthy share in the effective exertions of the *Hilfs-Verein*. The society, within a few months, collected and spent the greater part of 700,000 thalers. With it co-operated several minor societies, of which the Berlin Ladies' Society, under the patronage of the Queen, also raised and distributed 375,000 thalers. The total amount of money, provisions, and wearing apparel sent to East Prussia in those calamitous days is reckoned at no less than 2,000,000 thalers; and it is probably owing to this generous aid that no more than 8,000 were infected with typhus in the districts of Königsberg and Gumbinnen, and that only 1,000 died.

As your readers may be somewhat interested to know how my letters on the religious condition of Germany have been received in the country they endeavour to pourtray, it may not be amiss to say that, while contradicted in no paper I have seen, they have been honoured with the unqualified approval of the *Cologne Gazette*, the *facile princeps* of the German Press.

BERLIN, *September* 2, 1869.

CHAPTER IX.

PROTESTANT ASSOCIATION MEETING.—I.

SIMULTANEOUS with Parliament, the annual meeting of the German Protestant Association was opened in the not very suitable locality of a Berlin gymnastic hall. The use of ecclesiastical buildings having, by the King's officials at the head of the Church, been denied the society on account of their free-thinking propensities, they were obliged to fall back upon a profane structure, placed at their disposal by the Town Council. Unfortunately, the hall chosen is too large for the friends of the society at Berlin. It would seem that my former remarks on the indifference of the general public to the society's ends and aims will be borne out by the result of this year's meeting. At any rate, the reasons which left men apathetic formerly remain in full force. In yesterday's debates, as on previous similar occasions, the spokesmen of the society omitted to prove the alleged necessity, or to state the possible contents, of a religion deprived of the doctrine of redemption, and the theistic notions on which that doctrine rests. Yet it is evident that as it is the society's object to recover for some such religion the rationalistic majority of the educated classes, they must plainly define the nature of their teaching before they can make it go down. When God's interference in the affairs of this sublunary world, in the ordinary acceptation of the term, is denied, and the recovery of lost sheep for a new religion, nevertheless, advocated in the same breath, the public have a right to expect a plain and unmistakable account of the novel faith. How is an atheist to be converted by telling him that the Deity does not indeed influence the self-supporting machinery of the Universe, but that there is, nevertheless, something in that Deity, undefined and undefinable, which, after all, it would be as well to adore? The society, stripping God Almighty of the powers usually attributed to Him, makes His relations to the world so utterly different from what they were hitherto believed to be, that they ought to consider themselves obliged to state in so many words what they propose to leave Him. Religious subjects, it is true, are so delicate in their nature that no one can be blamed for never mentioning them to his neighbour; but those who deem themselves called upon to advert to them publicly, nay, to urge a sweeping reform of the Church, might as well vouchsafe us a clear and intelligible epitome of their opinions. But whether the society do not think the world sufficiently advanced to accept positive teaching at their hands, or whether they despair of inculcating religious tenets at the present period of prevailing indifference, they leave the most important items of the controversy to be settled in the future. Whatever their reasons, for this strange reserve, if they do not demonstrate why religion, and which religion, is necessary after the undeniable decline of the old faith, they must not be surprised at this sceptic generation turning a deaf ear to their entreaties to come and join them, or at the few remaining orthodox charging the society with beginning a contest without finishing it. I have dwelt the more upon this singular hesitation of a body, so active and enterprising in other respects, as it seems to me the characteristic feature of the movement.

Nor will the papers advocating the society's cause greatly benefit it by recommending it not on its own merits but as a means of combating orthodox influences on the people. In the Berlin *National Zeitung*, the leading organ of the cultivated and liberal middle classes in the Eastern provinces, we read the following significant lines :—

"Has religion really lost its hold upon educated man, and is its action—as we are told so often—really confined to exciting the illiterate for a few transient moments, and that by the most objectionable means? Public indifference is begotten of two causes : the conviction that the dogmas of the Church have been annihilated by science, and a feeling of false security with respect to the attacks and anathemas of the ecclesiastical reactionaries. This feeling of security is a complete delusion, as long as Church and State are linked together, and the one helps the other to hector it over the people. Philosophers and freethinkers, moreover, are, as a rule, mistaken as to the effect of their teachings on the masses. As yet no philosophy has become truly popular, nor will ever become so ... At any rate, though the masses may be capable of enlightenment, they are not yet enlightened. The Protestant Association is desirous of becoming a bridge which shall lead from intellectual servitude to intellectual freedom."

The writer of the above does not think it worth his while to contradict the alleged conviction of the instructed laity that religion has been annihilated by science. On the contrary, he grounds his prayer to the intelligent reader to interest himself in the Church on the sole argument that that institution will otherwise become the exclusive domain of orthodoxy, and succeed in infusing old-fashioned prejudices into the people. Were the public to act on his advice, they would have to endeavour to wrench the direction of the Church from His Majesty's orthodox officials to whom it is intrusted, and then use their newly-acquired power in harmony with the above "conviction." In other words, they would have to palm upon the people a diluted form of the old faith, to be maintained as long as the poor benighted creatures cannot be brought to see the futility of any faith whatsoever. But the public will do no such thing. Considering not only themselves, but also the lower classes as above being imbued with the religious notions of the past, they do not at all deem it needful to embark in an ecclesiastical feud with the Crown. They might some of them be recovered for a unitarian form of religion, were the society, strengthened as it is with the authority of the many eminent and highly respectable men in it, to advocate the adoption of such a creed; but from all such decisive steps the society as yet resolutely abstains. Very likely the *Vossische*

Zeitung, which of all Berlin papers has the largest circulation in Berlin, will be found right in its prediction that the society, now that it has met for the first time in this criticising capital, will either attract a large number of friends or go away with previous popularity impaired.

To return to the proceedings. The meeting was opened by Dr. Schwartz, chaplain to the Duke of Coburg-Gotha, preaching the inaugural sermon in an improvised pulpit, in the Gymnastic Hall. From his eloquent and well-rounded periods I will quote only the few following words:—

"We believe in Christ as an historical Personage whose image has been obscured by fantastic traditions, but whom we reverence as the pure and noble founder of the Church. We believe in the Gospel and its doctrine of all-embracing love as taught by Christ. We deny miracles, knowing the universe to be governed by fixed laws; but we recognise the wonders worked by the Spirit, we recognise the force of love and the hope beyond the grave. We protest against the assumption of our adversaries that in denying the arbitrary interference of God in the progress of mundane affairs we have abandoned our belief in a living God."

How the denial and the affirmation contained in the last sentence are to be reconciled together the Rev. Dr. Schwartz does not say. And yet this ought to have been the principal thing to explain, inasmuch as it is an evident and generally acknowledged fact that the majority of those steeped in atheism have been led into their lamentable perversion by first denying the "arbitrary interference of God." Before and after the sermon the congregation sang hymns avowing their faith in Christ and His Blood.

Dr. Bluntschli, Professor of Jurisprudence at Heidelberg, a distinguished and generally renowned politician, was then elected chairman of the meeting. In returning thanks, among other things, he said:—

"The ancient Church was based upon the notion of a subterranean hell, with demons, flames, &c. Science has done away with this grotesque fancy, as well as with all other fables, and the attempt now making to subject 19th century reason to 4th century superstitions will ever be futile. In these modern days there is not a peasant boy but knows better than to believe in those antiquated ideas. The time will come when religion and knowledge will be reconciled. It will come soon, and my sons, I trust, will live to see it. Were the orthodox party to come off victorious in the struggle, the Church would ultimately consist of professional clergymen preaching for bread, a good many hypocrites, and a handful of believers."

After this the assembly entered upon the discussion of the school question. The majority of the members reject the supervision practically exercised by the clergy over the elementary schools, and seem to be of opinion that the public educational institutions should be open to all denominations alike, though religious instruction might be imparted to the pupils of each denomination separately. This is in opposition to the Prussian Government, who, in the last thirty years, have favoured separate schools for each sect.

The occasion of the meeting has been improved by three famous preachers, members of the Verein, each giving a lecture on a theological subject. The elegant rooms selected for this purpose in a fashionable part of the town were crowded with large audiences, admitted gratis. Dr. Baumgarten, late Professor of Theology at Rostock, spoke of the duties of the Protestant Association with regard to its enemies. An earnest and devoted man, the Professor insisted that the letter killeth, but the spirit giveth life. The Rev. Dr. Schellenberg, from Mannheim, in a lecture on Isaiah, asserted the continuance of the gift of prophecy. According to him, Luther, Lessing, Schiller, Fichte, Schleiermacher, and Humboldt, by enlightening the world, have become the successors of the Jewish prophets of old. The Rev. E. Bulle, from Bremen, in a lecture entitled " Our right to remain in the Church," urged that "all Christ demands of us is Repentance and Faith. To act piously, therefore, not to think dogmatically, is the one thing needful. To enable the German Protestant people to make their Church what it ought to be, they must sever it from the State and invest the congregations with the right to arrange their own services." On to-day's debates I shall report in my next.

BERLIN, *October* 7, 1869.

CHAPTER X.

PROTESTANT ASSOCIATION MEETING.—II.

As on the first day of the meeting, so on the second, the proceedings of the Protestant Association opened by the performance of Divine Service. After the singing of Luther's "*Ein feste Burg,*" the Rev. Dr. Schiffmann, from Stettin, preached a most impressive sermon. He said :—

"Those convinced of the omnipresence of God Almighty might adore Him in a gymnastic hall as well as in a church. The Protestant Association aimed at reviving religion, respect for which had declined among the people. When Christ was on the earth the Jews did not lack priests and rabbis. They had Sadducees, Pharisees, and other self-constituted guardians of the faith, who prayed much, and offered sacrifice, in the temple of Jehovah. Yet they appeared to Christ as sheep having no shepherd. A similar want of real, heartfelt piety, notwithstanding all external devotion, had been noticeable in the Protestant Church of Germany during the last thirty years. By a certain party no sermon was now-a-days considered a Christian sermon unless the name of Christ occurred in it over and over again; no man accounted religious unless a member of several religious societies. With the persons he was alluding to it had become the fashion to promote the interests of the Church, and forget those of the kingdom of God. In opposition to these the Protestant Association endeavoured to preach the pure, simple, and unalloyed Gospel doctrine. He whose soul was accessible to the teachings of Christ needed no theology, no rules and regulations as laid down by the doctors of the Church to become good and pious. To acknowledge the greatness and love of God, to do His will, to repent and pray, was all that was inculcated by Jesus Christ. This great and important fact should be preached to those thousands who, ceasing to believe in ancient dogmas, fancied there was nothing left for them but to look upon all religion with indifference, and practically separate themselves from the Church. To win these back to the essential truths of Christianity the society had been set on foot. What other object, indeed, than to obey the dictates of their conscience could the members have? They had no reward to expect from the authorities of the Church, who disapproved their doings, nor from the public generally, who looked upon them with apathy and coldness. But they were labourers performing their allotted task, and caring nothing for praise or immediate success. They would continue their endeavours to bring to the people that blessedness which comes from the knowledge of Christ."

Delivered with great fervour and earnestness, this address was not without an edifying effect upon the audience. By only inculcating the broad doctrine of heartfelt piety, the preacher avoided the self-contradiction in which so many other members of the society entangle themselves, of first seemingly reducing God to a nonentity, and then enjoining faith in Him.

After this Professor Schenkel, from Heidelberg, held forth on the state of religion generally in Protestant Germany. It was the speech of the day, and worthy of the Professor's renown as a scholar, an orator, and a thoroughgoing rationalist. A few extracts will suffice:—

"Implicit belief in the letter of Holy Writ was dying out everywhere. Liberty of conscience was becoming equivalent to liberty of culture, in this, as in all other civilized States of the world. Even England, with her stolid adherence to ancient tenets, was beginning to realise the fact that the kingdom of God was not based on the Thirty-nine Articles and fat sinecures. The Spaniards gave signs of shaking off their rusty chains, and on the other side of the ocean, in the United States of America, a new culture was growing up on a soil richly prepared by the servants of free and unfettered religion. To sever the State from the Church, and subject it to the government of its members, was more necessary in Germany than anywhere else. Germany was the country of the Reformation, and would not hesitate to effect another Reformation, or even a revolution, to complete the good work. The time would come when those modern religious ideas which were already recognised by the upper classes, and had even penetrated to the lower strata of society, would become omnipotent. Until that came about, the parsons would continue to wrangle about dogmas, to the intense delight of Pope and Jesuit. They would continue to denounce the Protestant Association as a body of heretics, and make religion so unreasonable and unintelligible a thing that it was but too natural for weak and misguided understandings to leave Protestantism altogether and go over to Rome. The Hanover Church had actually had the hardihood to depose two clergymen for placing their names on the list of the Protestant Association. Who, on hearing of this deplorable act, could help remembering that once there existed a synod yclept 'the Synod of Robbers?' Unshaken by this and other attacks, the Association would abide by their conviction that the period of dogmatism had passed away, but that the root of religion was still alive, and would flourish for ever. He took the liberty of proposing the following theses for adoption by the meeting:—

"'I. The main cause of the dissension prevailing in the Evangelical Church of Germany, as well as its consequent weakness and openness to attack from Rome, is the policy of some German Governments to hinder the free development of its principles and vital force.

"'II. Instead of a Church directed by parsons and consistories, the nominees of the respective Governments, we demand a true German Church, under the control of the congregations. The so-called synods recently introduced into the six Eastern provinces of Prussia are mere sham concessions to the principle of self-government in the Church.

"'III. To restrict scientific inquiry, and confine the liberty of religious teaching within dogmatic limits, is to sap the foundation of that evangelical life whose only master is Jesus Christ, the Redeemer and perfecter of humanity.

"'IV. Firmly maintaining this the essential truth of the Protestant faith, we protest against the absolute rule of dogma, and the forcible imposition of religious teachings. Whoever should see in this our declaration a denial of the saving truths of Christianity, and, imitating the Pharisees, desire our exclusion from the Christian community, is guilty of sinning against the cardinal virtue of Christian morality—Love.

"'V. We repel and most determinately protest against the unproved accusations laid to the charge of our society by the authorities of the Prussian Church. We do not object to any dogmatic teaching, provided it co-operates with us in renewing and reviving the Church on its old imperishable basis, in a spirit of Gospel freedom, and in harmony with the civilization of the age.

"'VI. All German men who are of like opinion with ourselves are hereby again publicly and solemnly invited to join us in struggling against all un-Protestantistic and hierarchic aggression, and in protecting the right, the honour, and the liberty of German Protestantism.'"

Like most other utterances of the society, this speech was strangely reticent just where it ought to be most explicit. It denied the attributes of the Divinity as anciently understood, yet left it unexplained what its relations to the individual and the world at large are henceforth to be. This omission will be scarcely compensated for by the introduction of such terms as "Redeemer" and "saving truths of Christianity" into a rationalistic thesis, where they must necessarily mean something very different from the accepted sense. All the theses proposed were adopted.

Professor Schenkel was succeeded by several other speakers of name and fame. Professor Baumgarten, from Rostock, an orthodox Christian, said that he had joined the society because it vindicated the principle of disestablishment. The Rev. Dr. Schmidt called Christ to witness that there were plenty of hypocrites among the orthodox adversaries of the society. Professor Dr. Von Holtzendorf, the famous jurist and teacher of international law, moved for a resolution to the effect, that the repeal of capital punishment would not be contrary to Divine injunctions. The anti-decapitation movement having lately made considerable progress in the country, this resolution was carried pretty unanimously.* The singing of a hymn closed the proceedings of the day and of the meeting. The sittings had been attended by about three hundred members and from four hundred to five hundred visitors,—an inadequate number for such a large and stirring place as Berlin.

* On a recent occasion the Judges of the Berlin Criminal Court, being called upon to give an opinion on this much discussed question, nearly one half of them declared for the repeal of capital punishment. And still more recently—in March, 1870—the Federal Parliament passed a vote to the same effect, though they knew it would not be sanctioned by Government. At about the same time, the Second Baden Chamber declared in favour of the repeal; the First Chamber opposed the innovation, but only, because they did not think it opportune to introduce it before being ratified by the Northern Confederacy. One of the arguments used by the opposers to capital punishment is that intending criminals are not deterred by the fear of retribution, but always hope to remain undiscovered. Decapitation, therefore, not serving to diminish the number of murders, and being, moreover, unsuited to a civilised age, it ought to be done away with. To this reasoning the conservatives, and with them the Prussian Government, retort, that capital punishment is enjoined in the Bible, and that, as all punishments are a check, it follows that the severer the penalty the surer its effect.

BERLIN, *October* 9, 1869.

CHAPTER XI.

THE HUMBOLDT CENTENARY.

YESTERDAY the hundredth anniversary of the birth of Alexander von Humboldt, was celebrated at Berlin, his native city. Suitably to commemorate the day a public ceremony was arranged by the municipal authorities, which, occupying the morning, left the afternoon and evening free for other more private and exclusive festivities.

The public ceremony was held in the fields adjoining a poor and rather neglected suburb of this wide metropolis. It consisted in the planting the first tree of a park to be laid out for the benefit of the inhabitants of that humble neighbourhood, and to be named after the hero of the day. In addition to this the first symbolical commencement of the new Humboldt Park, a foundation-stone was laid for an unpretending monument to be erected in the same locality. A granite block, inscribed with Humboldt's name, is the simple memorial to be placed in the centre of the future pleasure grounds.

At ten o'clock A.M. the municipal officers and members of the Town Council betook themselves in solemn procession to the site of the commemorative park. They were followed by many artisans, divided according to their various trades, and marching with flags and banners, in the usual German style. Some other popular societies brought up the rear. The few professors and students—there are not many in Berlin during the long vacation—who might be seen hastening to the spot, were mostly in cabs, as the distance from the better quarters of the town was considerable, and the weather abominable. Of those sections of the higher and middle classes not professionally interested in science and literature, few representatives were perceived. The ladies, for whom an especial platform had been erected in the best place, could be easily counted.

The outskirts of the intended park were marked by poles bearing flags of varied hues and devices. In the centre stood a gigantic bust of Humboldt, surrounded by a perfect forest of palm trees. Immediately in front was dug the hole which was to receive the foundation-stone of the monument. Here were stationed in symmetrical lines the municipal authorities, the trades' societies, and the choral unions.

All round this nucleus of respectability surged the sea of the mixed population of the suburbs.

The singers having performed Beethoven's music to the psalm, " The Heavens declare the glory of God," the Burgomaster Seydel addressed the assembly in a brief and characteristic speech. He said:—

" They were celebrating the memory of one of the greatest men that had ever graced or benefited humanity. A genius in the walks of science, he was equally remarkable for his patriotism and the interest he took in the political and intellectual progress of his countrymen. His discoveries had eminently contributed to do away with the belief in miracles, and establish the truth that Nature was governed by immutable laws. Religious mythology had disappeared before the searching light of Reason, and what he had done, would continue to bear fruit and educate this people and the world generally."

After this speech, received in absolute silence, Herr Duncker, the syndic of the town, read the document to be enclosed in the foundation stone, which, in words of Tacitean compactness, recounts the merits of the distinguished scholar, and the resolution of the Town Council to honour his memory by the creation of a

Humboldt Park. The usual strokes of the hammer were then administered by Burgomaster Seydel, Field-Marshal Wrangel, Count Bismark Bohlen (the commandant of Berlin), Herr Reichenau (the chief superintendent of the Brandenburg schools), some liberally inclined clergymen, and three professors, respectively from Vienna, Leipsic, and Berlin. Before the stone was lowered, Burgomaster Seydel begged leave to communicate a congratulatory telegram he had just received from the Crown Prince and Crown Princess. In graceful sympathy with the event of the day, it ran:—

"Our cordial salutations to those that have met to keep the Humboldt centenary. By doing honour to her great fellow-townsman Berlin honours herself. A hero in the field of science, Humboldt was the friend and faithful servant of his King, and ever warmly sympathized with the welfare of the people. Few merit as he did the gratitude of his age, and of coming generations.

"FRIEDRICH WILHELM; VICTORIA."

Another song, semi-religious in character, accompanied the placing of the stone, upon which Herr Kochan, the chairman of the Town Council, uttered the closing oration. It was conceived in the same demonstratively rationalistic spirit as the inaugural harangue. Herr Kochan exclaimed :—

"Humboldt was the fittest representative of this enlightened and progressive age. By his brilliant discoveries in every department of natural science, he had paved the way for a more correct apprehension of this world and its glories. He had taught mankind to adore God in his works. The park they were about to form would give the inhabitants of this town another opportunity of admiring the Creator in the beauty of tree and shrub, independent of all dogmas and obliterated creeds. This was perfectly in unison with the pure and uncontaminated doctrine of Christ, though it might not agree with the absurd tenets propagated by haughty parsons, to the prejudice of religion and truthfulness. Those that considered themselves followers of Alexander von Humboldt should ever strive to eradicate superstition and ignorance."

During this speech the morning's drizzle had turned into a pouring rain. It was a dismal sight to see the passive multitude in the pelting shower. After three cheers for the King, the assembly, which, excepting the few customary attendant hurrahs, had from beginning to end evinced no visible or audible sign of interest, was but too glad to disperse.

Such was the public ceremony, which certainly did not come up to the importance of the event. The weather, it is true, was unpropitious, but other circumstances combined to mar the whole affair. Humboldt was a determined Liberal. The political opinions he uniformly expressed during his long and active life, and still more a curious revelation concerning them after his death, made the Court, Government, and aristocracy look coldly upon the ovation. Many of your readers may probably have heard of the intimate friendship which bound the illustrious naturalist to King Frederick William IV. Both were equally sensible of the pleasure derived from intellectual pursuits. Both were noble in character and poetical in taste. An early intimacy between them was continued beyond the period when the King, in the vicissitudes of the political struggle of his time, had turned Conservative. Humboldt continued to go to Court, even when he no longer agreed with his Royal friend on those numerous questions of political or philosophical learning, to discuss which together had in former days been their common delight. This intellectual rupture between the sovereign and the philosopher made the latter's position at Court an awkward one, and eventually left him no friend in the palace save the King. Since those days Frederick William IV. has been gathered to his ancestors, a new era has supervened, and Court and Government have become more tolerant than they were in that gloomy interval of Prussian history. If remembering at all the sarcasms the Liberal scholar would sometimes bandy about in the Royal chambers and antechambers, they would have scarcely thought fit to show their feelings on the centenary of a man of world-wide fame ; but an unfortunate revelation, made after his death, rendered it—it must be owned—rather difficult for them to let bygones be bygones, to exalt the naturalist and forget the politician. Humboldt's special friend was the famous Varnhagen, an eminent Prussian diplomatist, whom Liberal sentiments had deprived of his position in the public service, in which otherwise he would probably have reached the highest steps of the ladder. Varnhagen, who achieved a first-class literary reputation as the biographer of some Prussian statesmen and generals, had a natural talent for writing a diary, and collecting the small facts of everyday life which in their aggregate go far to make up history. During the long years he passed at Berlin without public employment, this irrepressible bent, together with the indignation he felt at the proceedings of the Government, led him to put down in black and white every word on politics he could glean from leading men in State and Church. His chief object being to delineate what he considered a pernicious system, you may easily imagine what his diaries are like. He had no sooner departed this life, when his niece, to whom his literary papers were bequeathed, thought it a duty she owed to her democratic friends to print sundry volumes of the dangerous stuff. In them, among many other things of the same nature, were found recorded numerous utterances of Humboldt which cannot but be very disagreeable to men still living and exercising no small influence. The first result of the publication was that the very name of Humboldt was tabooed by the Conservative party. Even many Liberals were at a loss how to reconcile Humboldt's continued attendance at Court with the things he, it now appeared, had whispered in his friend's closet against that Court. Indeed, from Varnhagen's jottings there can be no doubt that he did not think it necessary to avoid meeting and treating with the ordinary forms of polite intercourse persons whom he hated and despised in his heart. If he, nevertheless, went where he knew he would have to converse with them in a courteous manner, his motive probably was that he could not reach the King without stumbling upon his attendants. As to his feelings towards his Royal friend, there are numerous facts to prove they were not affected by the political estrangement between the two. Nay, that political estrangement itself was never very serious. Frederick William IV., a man of uncommon talent, was far too clever not to cherish many modern and enlightened opinions, even after his notions concerning the value of Constitutional Government had been modified to the extent of making him act mostly with the Conservatives. He never was an absolutist. He willingly submitted to that restriction of his Royal prerogative, which under the ancient arrangements of the country proceeded from the legitimate influence of an intelligent, honourable and independent bureaucracy; and if he thought that this mode of limiting the Royal power was more conducive to the people's welfare than Parliamentary Government, this, in the nineteenth century, was an error of judgment, but had nothing in common with a vulgar lust of power. Hence the King remained Liberal, generous, and refined in thought and feeling, though but too many of the men he had to employ for the furtherance of his conservative politics were the reverse. It is no wonder, then, that the relations between the Sovereign and the scholar were not altered by their opposite politics. But if Humboldt loved the King, whose motives he respected, though he did not approve his actions, he, in Varnhagen's closet, indemnified himself by free speech for the unpleasantness of compulsory intercourse with those political friends of his Sovereign whom he thought selfish, stupid, and coarse. The censure he then vented under the seal of friendship told against yesterday's anniversary. Court and Government scarcely noticed the day. Of the Royal family only the King and Crown Prince paid their tribute of respect to the deceased; the King by sanctioning the erection of a Humboldt statue in Berlin, and the Crown Prince and Crown Princess by sending the before-mentioned telegram. No Minister and, with one exception, no chief of a Government Board took part in the public ceremony; no Government office displayed a flag; the schools were not permitted to commemorate the day, and altogether the thing was evidently not countenanced by the powers that be.

But not Government alone, the higher and middle classes likewise ignored the day. The artisans turned out because they fancied, though wrongly, Humboldt was a democrat; the second and third rate streets near the new park were decorated with banners and garlands, as the festivities seemed to be got up for their especial benefit; but of well-to-do people few, if any, were there, except the scanty list given above, and scarcely a flag was to be discovered in the wealthier and more fashionable quarters. The truth is that the scientific merits of Humboldt are of a kind not to be easily appreciated even by the cultivated classes. Excepting a few volumes of secondary importance, a man to understand his works must himself be a scholar. But if it is difficult for ordinary minds to form an adequate idea of Humboldt's scientific deserts, it was all the more easy to foresee that his centenary would be turned into a mere rationalistic display by those, honouring him rather as a champion of general enlightenment, than as an able and minute inquirer into the mysteries of nature. For though his discoveries were all made in the field of abstract science, and have no immediate bearing upon the debatable questions in religion and politics, yet, as they extend to all branches of physical inquiry alike, and have so powerfully contributed to raise it to its present height, freethinkers of all hues and shades have long been in the habit of representing Humboldt as the most eminent exponent of this modern era, with its skill in analyzing the visible and its comparative indifference to the laws and hopes that govern the more mysterious action of the soul. Things fell out, as anticipated. The speakers at the ceremony harped upon the one note of rationalism, and no doubt to the delight of the working men around them. But the educated classes, it would seem, have heard the like sentiments too often to care for a repetition of them, however rhetorical. They knew what they had to expect, and in consequence shone by their absence. They certainly avow the truth of scientific inquiry, rationalism, and so on; but they are scarcely sufficiently satisfied by the influence those principles have thus far exercised upon their views of life, religion, and morality to be desirous of hearing them extolled again and again. In a word, they at this moment lack the connecting link between science and religion, and, while doing so, take no very earnest interest in either.

In the evening a number of private festivities had been arranged. The most attractive was that of the Geographical Society, which brought together about five hundred gentlemen, and was honoured with the presence of Dr. Bancroft, the American Envoy, alike distinguished as scholar and diplomatist, and some

Ministers of State. His Majesty had condescended to express his regret at being, by the military manœuvres, prevented from attending. Dr. Bastian, the ethnographical traveller, delivered an ardent and elaborate speech, somewhat contrasting with the sober tone of the meeting. The supper which succeeded was graced by numerous toasts in honour of the occasion. Professor Virchow communicated to the assembly the greetings of Baroness Gleichen, a daughter of Schiller, who to commemorate the friendship that bound her father to the deceased, sent a laurel wreath for Humboldt's bust. Herr von Ruthenow, an Austrian nobleman, deputed by the Vienna Geographical Society, amid universal applause, spoke in favour of that intellectual unity of all Germany which must be preserved, even were political reunion unattainable. Herr Löwenberg, a personal friend of Humboldt, thanked the town of Berlin for the honours it conferred upon the departed genius. These and many other speeches were appropriate enough, but being delivered, *more Germanico*, between the various dishes, kept people two hours hungry and five hours at table.

Another more popular meeting was held at Krolls, where artisans and tradesmen met to hear Humboldt praised by a Radical philosopher. The middle classes, absent in the morning, were equally undemonstrative in the evening. Whether the similar social gatherings which came off at Leipsic, Dresden, Munich, Vienna, Prague, Teplitz, and many other German and Austrian towns were a success has not yet been reported. The papers abounded with glowing leaders beforehand.

The centenary has suggested two interesting books. The one just out is a collection of Humboldt's letters to Chevalier Bunsen, the late Prussian Ambassador in London. The contents are mostly political, displaying the well-known liberalism of the writer, who knew his sentiments were cordially reciprocated by his correspondent. The other book is a biography, to be published shortly under the direction of Professor Bruhn, at Leipsic. The plan upon which it is to be written is as unique as the man whose portrait it undertakes to give. It will be composed by twelve Professors, each describing Humboldt's achievements in that particular branch of natural science to which he has specially devoted himself. One man suffices not to describe this one.

BERLIN, *September* 15, 1869.

CHAPTER XII.

A DAY OF PRAYER AND HUMILIATION.

REGARDING with anxious solicitude the religious controversy going on in the country, the King three weeks ago issued the following decree, appointing a day of Prayer and Humiliation :—

" The great movements which in our age are making themselves felt in the religious life both of nations and individuals and are pressing forward to a decision, and the tasks they impose on the Protestant Church of our country, are apparent to all, and admonish us to entreat the support of Almighty God. It is therefore my will that a day be set apart in the Protestant Churches of my country for special prayer that God may pour out his blessing on the present important deliberations as to the constitution of our Church, and to implore Him to protect the Protestant Church from all dangers that threaten it, and to strengthen the ties which unite its members to each other and to the Church universal. I have appointed the 10th of November, the birthday of

Dr. Martin Luther, for this purpose, and hereby commission the Minister, and the highest ecclesiastical authorities of Prussia, to make the necessary arrangements.

"WILLIAM."

"BADEN-BADEN, *Oct.* 21, 1869."

I am afraid I cannot say the metropolitan churches were fuller on November 10th than on ordinary occasions.

BERLIN, *November* 12, 1869.

CHAPTER XIII.

THE PRUSSIAN GOVERNMENT AND THE ESTABLISHED CHURCH.

YESTERDAY and to-day Herr von Mühler, the Minister of Ecclesiastical and Educational Affairs, has been again set upon by the Liberals in the Lower House. The Budget of his particular Department being brought up for discussion, not a few members profited by this rare opportunity for telling the Minister what the immense majority of educated men in the country think of him. His Excellency, as I have had occasion previously to observe, is the avowed antagonist of the latitudinarian views lately prevalent in this part of the world. In this respect many good, pious, and enlightened men agree with him, or, if not, are, at any rate, imbued with sufficient reverence for religion in the abstract to be able to appreciate the motives which urge him to contend for the old form of faith. But the arms he employs in the great spiritual battle of the day are generally thought not to be the most suitable for this latter half of the nineteenth century. Herr von Mühler, who practically, though not nominally, is the chief of the Established Church, designs to cure the intellectual disease of the age by unreasoning belief in the letter of the Bible, and is all in favour of the strong secular arm for carrying out his purpose. A strict creed which shall pronounce dogmatically even on the minute details of sacred mysteries, and shut out entirely the light of modern science, is the medicine he prescribes for his benighted countrymen: and if they will not swallow it willingly, as many as circumstances permit him to coerce are made to feel that it must be gulped down somehow. The classes undergoing this forcible process are the clergy, the teachers in public and private schools, and the scholars themselves. By the clergy not much resistance has been as yet offered him. On the contrary, many Protestant ministers, frightened by the ever-increasing strength of disbelief around them, have cordially adopted the views of their secular chief, and are zealously co-operating with him in the Sisyphean task he has dauntlessly imposed upon himself. All the more dissatisfied with his measures are the teachers, the University professors, and the educated Laity at large. Leaving alone for the present the scholastic profession, whose grievances

will be explained in a special letter, we find the upper
classes adhering to notions diametrically opposed to
those of the minister and his ecclesiastical friends.
In proportion as belief in the letter of Holy Writ
has been insisted upon as the primary duty of man,
the churches have become emptier, until, broadly
speaking, they are attended only by the few sharing
these strict opinions, and the uneducated, whose religion is one of feeling and habit rather than reflection.
In Berlin, for instance, most of the Churches are invariably empty, although the accommodation provides
only for 25,000 out of a population of 800,000. However little they may have intended it, it is a fact that
the spread of Rationalism, instead of being stopped
by the clergy reverting to orthodox views, has been
indirectly promoted by the many uncompromising
reverend gentlemen ranging themselves on this side
the question. Determined latitudinarians are, of
course, too far gone to be easily recovered by clergymen who look upon them as lost and undone;
but even people of more moderate views, with a
residue of religious sentiment left, who by more congenial instructors might be gained back to a positive form of religion, are alienated by the excessive
discrepancy between the ordinary compass of their

thoughts and the demands made upon them. People of this wavering class I have often heard say, that though to deserve its name religion must certainly define the relation between God and man, yet if it put forth positive statements on our connection with the Almighty, clashing with science and common sense, it cannot be the form of faith required for a reasoning age. Hence, the unpalatable lessons inculcated by the clergy find as little favour in the eyes of the public, as the more modern but vague and indefinite generalities of the Protestanten-Verein: the truth, it is thought, must be somewhere between the two opposite doctrines, of which the one pretends to know too much and the other is content with having to say too little on a subject which ought to be the chief concern of every rational being.

The ecclesiastical régime which has been unable to obviate such painful consequences is, moreover, in the eyes of the Liberals, based upon a forced and altogether unjustifiable interpretation of the law. By the Prussian Charter enacted in 1850 the Established Church was made independent of the State, and became free to administer its own affairs. Instead of, as was expected from this enactment, leaving the congregations to look after themselves, the King, in his ancient capacity as *membrum præcipuum* of the Church, re-appropriated the ecclesiastical power of which the charter had deprived him as the Sovereign of the land. The spiritual attribute thus claimed by the King is certainly in accordance with a principle acknowledged by Luther himself in his latter days, when the necessity of providing a fit government for the unruly believers of his age made him confer the privilege of Church supervision upon the various Protestant Sovereigns of Germany; but if it held good then, it is none the less at variance with modern views, and, far from being confirmed in the charter, has—at any rate, as the Liberals read that document—been expressly contradicted in it. But, say what they might, the Crown put its own construction on the clause in question, and from sheer indifference Parliament omitted to couch a formal protest. The upshot of the whole affair was that the Crown continued to reign supreme over the clergy, and that Parliament, which but for the nominal disestablishment pronounced in the charter, would have shared the legislative prerogative in the ecclesiastical as in every other department of the public administration, was denied the right of intermeddling with the "independent Church." This very peculiar arrangement the Crown, it is true, itself considered

K

provisional; yet it has never been altered. Since first imposing it the King has controlled the Church, not as King, but as *membrum præcipuum;* not in conjunction with Parliament, but alone as supreme ecclesiastical dignitary; not through his Minister of Ecclesiastical Affairs, who, being an officer of the State, cannot serve a spiritual chief, but through a clerical Consistory, absolute and omnipotent, called the Ober-Kirchen-Rath. From what I have said above I need not tell you that the Consistory is virtually appointed by the Minister, whose influence in the Establishment accordingly remains as great as it was in ante-constitutional times. Yet I do not know whether, but for Herr von Mühler, the Liberals would have been ever very loud in uttering any indignation at this extraordinary mode of reform. In all that regards religion public opinion has long been so very apathetic in this country that for years people scarcely cared to inquire who appointed the clergy and with whom rested the power to depose them. It was only the energetic use Herr von Mühler made of his authority in fomenting orthodox tenets which induced people to take again an interest in the Church, and after a time caused them to hiss and groan where formerly they had been mute and indifferent spectators.

Within the last few weeks their dissatisfaction has been raised to an uncommon height by certain novel proceedings of their Ministerial adversary. It must be owned, he is as fearless as he is incautious. Not satisfied with resting the supreme government of the Protestant faith upon what, in the most charitable view of the case, is a venturesome construction of an ambiguous phrase, his Excellency has now been pleased to employ an analogous method to endow the Church with Synods. With a view to establish a sort of connection between the absolutistic government of the Church and the congregations representative assemblies were some time ago instituted in the various parishes and dioceses of the old provinces. They had no right to decide, but only to advise; the lay members among them were elected by the congregations, but only out of a list of candidates presented by the clergy; and their sphere of action practically extended to only the most trifling, and, so to say, local items of Divine service. By these local Synods the Minister has now caused Provincial Synods to be elected, which at this moment are discussing matters of wider importance, and, entering as they do upon the delicate topics of creed, Prayer Book, and the like, necessarily attract some attention. What nobody had troubled himself to do before, the peculiar mode of forming these assemblies is being looked into by the public. The theories propounded by their members are examined, and the idea of creating institutions so novel in their composition, so antiquated in their aim, is criticised. What colour these remarks assume it would be superfluous to dilate upon. If Herr von Mühler did not consider it natural and even imperative upon him to regard those who are of his own way of thinking as the only true members of the Church, he would certainly have taken care not to show the people so openly that their Church at present belongs to the clergy—an absolutely governed clergy, too—but not to them. If I am rightly informed, the inexpediency of his proceedings in this particular case has been sufficiently noticed in the Cabinet and the spheres immediately above it to render the speedy dissolution of the Provincial Synods extremely probable. Meanwhile there are about a dozen of them stirring up the country to religious agitation, and provoking Parliament to treat the Minister who has convened them as no Minister of the Prussian Crown ought to be treated. The excess of his zeal is also shown in another significant instance. Some of your readers may be aware that the Established Church of

Prussia is a compromise between the Lutheran and Calvinistic creeds, and, as such, attaches comparatively inferior importance to those disputed points about the Real Presence which so long kept the two Protestant denominations of the Continent asunder. Now Herr von Mühler, though practically at the head of the Established Church, happens to be more orthodox than the institution intrusted to his care, and has long favoured the tendency of those of the clergy who, more or less openly oppose the compromise between the two kindred creeds, and endeavour to supersede the Established religion by returning to the Old Lutheran and Old Reformed faiths. The Old Lutherans especially, as they believe in the letter of Holy Scripture, and assert Christ to be bodily present in the bread and wine, have ever been the Minister's favourites. Having shown this predilection in Prussia Proper before the late annexations, he has since been only too happy to evince it in the new provinces, where the Lutheran creed is the established one. That those men in the new provinces most eager in keeping up the Lutheran creed are not only ultra-orthodox in religion, but also ultra-Conservative in politics, and consequently adherents of their dethroned dynasties, has been too worldly a consideration to be taken into account by Herr von Mühler. In Hanover, for instance, where a considerable portion of the clergy are Old Lutherans and Old Guelphians into the bargain, the Prussian Minister of Church and Educational Affairs was so enchanted with their religious tendencies as to entirely overlook their politics, and place the elementary schools under their exclusive control—a thing nowhere else done, either in the new or old parts of the country. Instead of being grateful for this, the Hanover clergy, in their present Synod, have raised the question whether a Prussian King, being of the Established religion of the old Monarchy, has the right to take cognizance of anything that concerns the Lutheran Church of Hanover, except, of course, the rendering all needful assistance by the *bracchium seculare*.

Berlin, *December* 1, 1869.

CHAPTER XIV.

THE SCHOOLS AND THE ESTABLISHED CHURCH.

HOWEVER much the public mind was engrossed by the Church debate, it is even more intensely excited by the School question, now under discussion in the Lower House. No wonder it is so. The influence Herr von Mühler, the Minister of Church and Educational Affairs, exercises on things ecclesiastical is certainly wielded in a more orthodox spirit than educated men desire; nay, it is of a more rigorous and uncompromising cast than the teaching of Luther himself, who, it is well known, did not believe in the literal inspiration of all the books of the Bible, and even declared some of them to be the product of ordinary human writers. Still, as few people go to church now-a-days, the public suffer no direct inconvenience from the pulpit being, in accordance with Ministerial mandate, made the vehicle for the propagation of doctrine considered antiquated as far back as the time of the great Reformer; and if the injury people indirectly sustain from being kept out of the churches by uncongenial teaching is formidable and cannot be regarded in too serious a light, this is a circumstance not so generally felt at a period but too much inclined to neglect spiritual for temporal concerns. But the defects in the educational system are brought home to every household. In Prussia public and private schools alike are controlled by the Minister presiding over that department. In all of them must be taught whatever he is pleased to prescribe, without either parents or teachers having any voice in the matter, or being allowed to appeal to a higher and less arbitrary authority. Hence, whoever cannot afford to have his children privately instructed in his own house is obliged to submit to their being brought up according to the plan laid down by Government. Under these circumstances it cannot be a matter of indifference to parents that the Government — represented in the present instance by Herr von Mühler — should have latterly forced upon the schools a severe form of orthodoxy, which is rejected even by numbers uninfected by the fashionable taint of rationalism. Enlightened fathers of families have to shake their heads in dismay at seeing religious instruction chiefly confined to mystical details altogether beyond the grasp of the youthful intellect. Mothers may be heard to complain that certain subjects, which modern orthodoxy makes it a point not to shrink from, are brought too prominently forward before their little ones. And both fathers and mothers have for some years had but too much occasion to regret that the method employed in acquainting their sons with sacred things should mainly consist in making them learn by heart a greater quantity of texts, hymns, and biblical stories than could be digested by the children, even did they understand them. If the protests of parents have not been louder, it is not for want of dislike to the system. The fact is that religious training, as imparted by the Minister's fiat, is in too glaring discrepancy with the prevailing views of the age to make any impression on the children. Being aware that Herr von Mühler is vainly employed in filling the Danaides' bucket, the parents are content not to disturb him in his futile task. They, indeed, lament that so much precious time should be consumed in communicating to their children that which they themselves regard as useless and do not hesitate to tell them is untrue; but they have slight apprehension that the "Old World tales" the boys hear at school will take root. As, moreover, the scientific instruction given in the higher educational institutions remains as excellent as ever, parents upon the whole think they can afford to smile at the Ministerial attempt to imbue the youthful mind with religious notions opposed to their own. It is only on occasion of Parliamentary debates, such as have been held the last few days, that the contrast between official and popular views is distinctly felt and resented.

The preceding remarks refer to the Grammar-schools and other superior establishments in which the youth of the country are prepared for the higher walks of life. Much worse is the effect of the Mühler system on the elementary schools, where the children of the lower classes imbibe their little item of knowledge to guide them through life's wearisome journey. In the case of these humbler nurseries of learning the new system is not confined to the religious lessons, but extends to all lessons alike. As early as 1854 Herr von Raumer, a member of the Manteuffel Cabinet, upon which devolved the task of putting down the radical hankerings which had manifested themselves so rudely in the movement of 1848, caused a new plan of instruction to be drawn up for the primary schools. His main object was to quench the enlightened, independent, and inquisitive spirit fostered under the scholastic system till then pursued. Somehow this Minister had conceived the idea that the lower classes had a better education than was wholesome for them, and that but for this egregious mistake of their rulers the troubles of 1848 would not have occurred. So he resolved upon a radical reform, and recklessly set to to change an order of things which it had cost a century to rear, which had grown a distinctive feature of the land, and which, by the common consent of the civilised world, had been a principal means of bracing up this people to pass unhurt through many a serious political crisis. Since then the Raumer *régime* has prevailed in the elementary schools. Bad enough as it was, it remained for Herr von Mühler to develop its injurious qualities still more fully, and render it the bane it is. At present instruction in natural science, history, and geography is reduced to a *minimum* in elementary schools. Practically, the children learn little beyond reading, writing, ciphering, and very many hymns and texts. Of these four subjects, hymns and texts have in the lower classes the greatest number of lessons devoted to them, while in both lower and higher forms nearly two-thirds of all that is committed to memory is religious matter.

According to a statement which has recently appeared in the papers, and remains uncontradicted, the children in the rural schools of the Gumbinnen district, where this injudicious system has reached its acme, are made to devote nearly four times as many hours to religious matter as to reading and writing. That orthodoxy has been promoted among villagers and artisans, by thus taking from them the modicum of science communicated under the former plan of instruction, no one acquainted with Prussia will assert; that religion has been effectively inculcated by a method addressing itself to the memory rather than the understanding and the heart, I have never seen stated; but it is admitted on all sides that mental culture has suffered. If the leaven of knowledge had not by a century of good instruction permeated the public mind too thoroughly to be neutralized by twenty years' bad schools, the consequences of the Raumer-Mühler method would be even more visible than they are.

Simultaneously with this transformation of the elementary schools was effected a corresponding reform of the seminaries in which the teachers are trained. Formerly the pupils of these seminaries received a tolerably liberal education. They learnt sufficient to enable them to realise the moral dignity of knowledge and infuse the like sentiment into the youthful mind. At present they are denied this lofty privilege of their calling. Rightly judging that no particular culture is wanted to render a man a mere teacher of the alphabet and a reciter of texts, Herr von Raumer had the training of the elementary schoolmaster ground down to a pattern quite on a par with the low requirements of his future calling. Now-a-days seminarists are permitted to know but little of natural science, geography, history, poetry, and logic, their time being chiefly taken up in repeating by rote an overpowering number of those hymns, texts, and Biblical extracts, to hammer which into the children's heads is to be the chief occupation of their lives. All mental food not in absolute accordance with the verbal interpretation of the Bible is prohibited within the walls of the seminary; every method tabooed, which could initiate pupils in the historical development of early Christianity. These principles are carried so far that the young candidates are strictly forbidden to read Göthe, Schiller, or any of those modern classics, the boast of the nation; while on the other hand there is so little done to accustom them to make use of their brains that mathematics are frequently taught in the seminaries on a novel system, specially invented to make them as mechanical as this the most logical of sciences will admit of. Have the teachers been rendered more orthodox by this meagre diet? At their last general meeting at Berlin a unanimous voice declared against what they denounced as an absolutely pernicious course.

That this opinion is shared by all classes of society, down to the very lowest, we have the melancholy satisfaction of being able to prove by undeniable statistics. It is an old story that elementary teachers in Prussia are underpaid. Only that love for their office which has so long distinguished them as a class could reconcile these useful members of society to the sacrifices it entails, and supply candidates for vacancies. Formerly many a teacher's son, while enduring the inconveniences of want under the paternal roof, yet became so deeply impressed with the beauty of the scholastic vocation as to make it a life's ambition to become his father's successor. Now, neither teachers' sons nor any others are particularly anxious for the honour. Who can blame them? What, not to speak of present poverty and the absence of future prospects, is there so attractive in this unprofitable profession, that should incline a man to forfeit his dignity by having to inculcate what he does not approve?

It is but natural that in the last six years there should have been noticeable a constantly increasing dearth of elementary teachers. Eventually it became so sensibly felt that, to keep the schools open, Government was obliged to have recourse to a sort of recruiting system, unheard of in the scholastic department of any country, and doubly odious in a land where, till within a short time ago, the position even of the elementary teacher had been considered a highly-respectable one. The teachers officiating in primary schools were actually offered a premium for each young man they could entice into the profession. The mere proposal of this expedient raised an outcry in the profession; and though a few recruits were caught under the new system, it did not answer to anything like the extent required. Other means, therefore, had to be employed. Abandoning all hope of enlisting men of any degree of cultivation, however slight, Government at last thought themselves compelled to seek for candidates among the humblest classes of society. In a word, Government, a couple of years ago, began converting field-hands and artisans into village schoolmasters. Not to alarm these children of nature by too much preliminary study, the course of instruction in the seminaries, ordinarily fixed at five and six years, in their case was cut down to little more than ten months. Already some hundreds of villages are provided with professors hatched under this novel process. But the worst of it all—or rather the best of it—is, that, notwithstanding the sorry tactics stooped to, the need of elementary teachers is as great as ever. There are at this moment nearly three thousand vacancies waiting to be filled up.

These are serious facts. In order to teach a form of religion which in the present intellectual state of the country does not impress the youthful mind, but, on the contrary, absolutely blunts it to a sense of all religion, Government have suffered national education to retrograde from that high excellence, the result of a century's continued efforts, the glory of three great Sovereigns. Government ought to consider that by prolonging this state of things they are rousing a spirit of opposition in the people which may eventually render it difficult for them to retain their prized right of control over the schools. I say Government ought to consider this, not Herr von Mühler, as, of all men, he is sure not to give in. Although all Liberal members in the House are unanimously against him, although but few Conservatives can be found venturesome enough to undertake his defence,

The Schools and the Established Church. 145

although, worst of all, the Ultramontanes are his only real adherents, he has just submitted a Bill expressly designed to perpetuate the system. It is anticipated that the House of Deputies will reject it *in toto*.

I must not close this letter without alluding to the painful discrepancy between the teaching of the Universities and that of the grammar-schools. The moment a young man is promoted from the Gymnasium to the College, his religious atmosphere is entirely changed. In the Gymnasium the strictest orthodoxy prevailed ; in the College—unless, indeed, his study is theology— he will not fall in with many professors whose lessons do not evince rationalistic tendencies. Now it may be more easy to regulate the grammar-schools than the Universities, which are the pride and glory of the land, and give it its intellectual tone ; but how can a youth be expected to reverence religion when, directly he emerges from the severe training of boyhood, his new masters teach him to look upon all his former lessons as mere food for babes and infants ? Is not this precipitous change of itself enough to upset religious belief for life ?

BERLIN, *December* 4, 1869.

CHAPTER XV.

THE SYNODS.

A FEW days ago the King received a deputation from the Brandenburg Synod, now sitting at Berlin, and, in reply to a loyal address, expressed himself as follows :

"I am much obliged to you for your kind and cordial wishes, and shall be happy to see you finish your work in peace. It is very necessary, indeed, that something should be done to quiet the excitement lately prevailing in matters ecclesiastical. The enemies of the Church are numerous in these days. In this I am not alluding to the Roman Catholics, but to those who have ceased to believe. What is to become of us if we have no faith in the Saviour, the Son of God ? If He is not the Son of God, His commands, as coming from a man only, must be subject to criticism. What is to become of us in such a case ? I can only repeat that I wish to see you finish in peace the work in which you are engaged."

This closed the audience. The work imposed on the Provincial Synod and referred to by the King is chiefly that of sanctioning the way in which its members are elected by the district Synods, those of the district Synods by the parish Synods, and those of the parish Synods by—the clergy. It may be strange, that the whole complicated ecclesiastical representative system, as newly established, should be based upon the nominees of the parish ministers. But so it is; for, although the parish Synods, from which the others issue, are chiefly composed of lay members elected by the congregations, none can be returned unless nominated by the local preachers. To sanction this peculiar sort of ecclesiastical franchise, recently imposed by the Crown, and also to declare that the right to advise the King is all that should be vested in those different assemblies, the provincial Synods have now been convoked, and, being practically appointed by the clergy, naturally expressed themselves highly gratified that this same arrangement is to continue. But these ecclesiastical votes are making some noise in the country, causing the King to apprehend that the work will not be finished in peace. Though to the great majority of the people everything occurring within the pale of the Church is such a matter of indifference that even these novel Convocations would of themselves have failed to impress them, there are those who have directed public attention to the subject. The Protestanten Verein has taken the field against the Synods. Made up of men rejecting the ancient creeds, yet sufficiently religious to long for some new Church, this society is strenuously opposed to the forcible means employed by the clergy of the Establishment in maintaining their views and position in the State. Accordingly their protests against the composition and votes of the Synods are loud and numerous. To give you an idea of the energy with which this small but wealthy, educated, and respected portion of society pronounces against those Synods which the King, in the confiding honesty of his heart, hopes are destined to remove existing difficulties, I will quote a few lines from a speech delivered at the last meeting of the Berlin branch of the Verein. The meeting was convened to protest against the "arbitrary composition" of the Synods. Before passing some telling resolutions to this effect, it attentively listened to an address from Professor von Holtzendorff, in which were the following passages:—

"In the provincial Synods were assembled all the most eminent clergymen of the Established Church. All very orthodox, and many of them highly intellectual, their debates had nevertheless only served to display the emptiness and hollowness of the present

Church. If the members of the Synod had been sitting in a Byzantine Council of the sixth century they could not have more thoroughly ignored the results of modern science and thought than they had done. All their wisdom had not sufficed to enlighten them as to what the religious convictions of the Prussian people are, and in what manner their religious wants ought to be satisfied. Not the ancient creeds, but love to God and our neighbour, is, in this age, considered the one thing needful. To try to uphold the creeds by force, and thereby practically shut out the congregations from the churches, as is done by the Government, is a terrible mistake, and cannot but inflict the severest injury upon the State. Had Prussia been defeated in 1866, and lost a portion of her territory, it would have been easier to bear than if the victor, instead of taking land, had imposed it as a condition of peace that the Prussian Church should be governed in the style it now is."

These sentiments were all warmly applauded by the meeting. I believe there are those among the clergy, even among the most orthodox portion of it, who do not deny that Synods elected in so peculiar a way, cannot be regarded as fairly representing the laity, for whose benefit they were formed. But, the clergy will ask, how is it possible to accord a less restricted franchise to the laity when the majority never attend Divine service, and, if allowed a vote, would only use it to the detriment of one and all of our sacred institutions? No one can deny the force of this objection. Were the people who have ceased going to church sufficiently religious to ask for some other settled form of faith than the one handed down to them, the clergy might be led to consider the possibility of a compromise; as it is, and while a pious wish for ecclesiastical reform is entertained by only a small minority, the clergy would not only ruin themselves, but also the Church, were they to allow it to be governed by the congregations. Perhaps if the more earnest members of the Protestanten Verein were to tell us not only which portions of the ancient creeds they reject, but also which they retain, a standard might be set up around which others would gather, and which the clergy, or at least a portion of it, would still regard as Christian, so as to be able to concede to its adherents the right to have a voice in Church affairs. In the meantime it is very true that none in Prussia have less to do with the Church than the congregations. What the Synods are we have seen above: in what way the clergy who appoint the Synods are themselves chosen will be seen from the following figures, which refer to the ecclesiastical statistics of the province of Brandenburg. In this province, a good specimen of the others, there is a Protestant population of 2,598,000 souls, belonging to 2,387 parish churches. In these churches officiate 1,317 clergymen, appointed for life, assisted by, I believe, a small number of curates. Of the 1,317 with a life interest in their preferments only four are elected by the congregations, while 555 are appointed by the ecclesiastical authorities, 56 by the King, 213 by Town Councils, and 489 by the proprietors of large estates acting in behalf of village communities. Of the clergy thus appointed, 56 members sit in the Brandenburg provincial Synod by the side of 51 laymen nominally elected by the district laity, and 23 other laymen deputed by the King.

It must not be passed over in silence that, true to their ancient politics, the orthodox clergy at the Synods betrayed a marked predilection for the re-introduction of absolute government. By the Liberals this is regarded as another proof that the clergy appreciate only that which is obsolete.

BERLIN, *December* 8, 1869.

CHAPTER XVI.

THE TRIAL OF CARL BILAND.

On the 12th instant young Biland was tried by Judge Luty, at the Berlin Criminal Court, on the charge of attempting to shoot the Rev. Dr. Heinrici while performing Divine service in the Cathedral. As the reader may remember, Biland is an atheistic fanatic, who looks upon Christianity as an egregious mistake, and the clergy as paid cheats. To avenge himself upon them for keeping him in the dark, and awaken his countrymen to a sense of their intellectual bondage, he had recourse to the pistol. Strangely anomalous as regards the criminal length to which he carried them, his views are too widely disseminated to be looked upon as the fallacies of a single wrong-headed individual, and dismissed accordingly. In young Biland we have a strong case of a very general malady. A little reflection made this clear even to our apathetic rationalists. People, indeed, are not yet prepared to resort to the unpalatable medicine of serious and humble-minded reflection, which alone can effect a cure; yet the sight of the disease in an extreme form naturally set many a one a-thinking, and secured a larger share of public attention to the trial, than was elicited by the committal of the crime. I believe, therefore, I shall be doing no work of supererogation in giving you the following brief account of what came out at the trial.

Born in 1851 at the village of Lank, county of Barnim, near Berlin, Carl Ludwig Otto Biland is the son of a blacksmith, and from his fifth to his tenth year attended the village school. Remarkable for quickness and industry, he attracted the attention of a neighbouring millowner, who, from his tenth to his thirteenth year, permitted the intelligent boy to share the private instruction imparted to his own sons. Three more years were spent in a Berlin grammar school, the father scraping together the little he had to complete his son's education, and make him, as he ambitiously hoped he might be, a teacher, or even a clergyman. While at school in Berlin the boy astonished his masters by his rapid progress, and, besides the tasks allotted him, greedily read whatever fell into his hands. Goethe, Schiller, Kant, and quantities of English and French novels he seems to have devoured at an age when such food was sure to be too much for his mental digestion. It was, however, long before his religious convictions, which from his infancy had been strictly orthodox, received any rude shock. For years, while studying Kant and other more rationalistic authors, he would regularly attend Divine service on Sundays, and write out afterwards the sermons he heard. Eventually, however, his religious belief was impaired, and, being an earnest and conscientious boy, he declared to his father that he felt unable to enter upon any vocation in which it would be his duty to teach the dogmas of Christianity. By much persuasion his father induced him to reconsider his resolve, and prepare himself for the career of an elementary schoolmaster. After another half-year's study, failing to pass his examination, he found himself shut out from the seminary, and returned home not dispirited, but rather elated at what he thought a lucky escape. He now determined to become an actor, that he might, as he said, preach poetical truth from the stage. His father objected, but, the son threatening to commit suicide, he at last gave in, and suffered him once more to betake himself to Berlin. Here he associated with actors and practised elocution; but, to his bitter disappointment, found no encouragement from adepts in the art. Whatever were the qualifications wanting, his histrionic friends were convinced he would never make his fortune on the stage. While cast down under these rebuffs he received a visit from his father, who conjured him to return to his studies, and fit himself for the more respectable and useful calling originally intended for him. His despair, coupled with filial affection, made him listen to the paternal representations, so that he promised again to take to his books. To carry out this intention he accompanied his father to Lauk, where he stayed a few weeks, bitterly repenting his promise and irresolute how to act. In this unsettled condition of mind it was that he conceived the idea of shooting a clergyman. He went to Berlin, cast a ball from a tin medal in honour of the Schiller centenary, and with this missile, sacred to the memory of his great favourite, committed the deed.

On the Judge addressing to him the ordinary question whether he pleaded guilty or not guilty, the poor misguided youth had the hardihood to reply:—" Not guilty. Being convinced that man is not a free agent, I cannot be guilty." To the question whether his religious views had anything to do with the attempt, he answered,—" I determined to shoot a clergyman because it is the clergy who have kept me so long in the dark. When studying mathematics I learnt to reason and emancipate myself from the untruths they taught me. There is no God. Nature is a self-supporting machine." When the Judge told him that he had misunderstood Kant and the classical poets he loved so dearly, he retorted :—" I have endeavoured to understand them to the best of my ability. I am convinced my opinions are based upon theirs. It was while witnessing the performance of Goethe's *Faust* and Schiller's *Räuber* that the idea of shooting a clergyman first occurred to me. When I levelled my pistol at the Rev. Dr. Heinrici, as he stood before the altar reciting the Creed, I bore no personal illwill to him. He was a clergyman, consequently a deceiver, and that was enough for me. I wished to make an example of one of the cloth, and was ready to abide the consequences. I will not, however, deny that my opinions have been somewhat modified since. If I were at liberty now, I should not repeat the act. I have learnt to understand that the shooting one of them is of no use at all." All which this daring boy of eighteen preferred with the utmost composure, smiling with philosophical equanimity, and meeting the searching interrogatories of the Judge with a calmness worthy of a better cause. Even when the jury found him guilty and the Judge sentenced him to twelve years of imprisonment, with hard labour, his courage, evidently the result of deep-rooted conviction, did not forsake him for a moment.*

The Rev. Dr. Kayser, a Catholic military chaplain at Düsseldorf, has been suspended from office by the Bishop of Cologne, for uniting in marriage the Prince of Roumania and the Princess of Wied, a Protestant lady, when neither he nor she were in a position to promise that their issue should be brought up in the Catholic faith. Reigning over a Greek orthodox people, the Prince, though a Roman Catholic, intends to have his children baptized in the religion of his subjects. The first priest he applied to refused point-blank, and it was only after some delay that his father, who resides at Düsseldorf, induced a clergyman of his acquaintance to perform the ceremony.

BERLIN, *December* 18, 1869.

* Five months after his sentence he was released from prison, and permitted to return to his parents, being in the last stage of consumption.

CHAPTER XVII.

THE LUTHER MONUMENT AT WORMS.

THE city in which Luther, pleading before the Sovereign and the assembled Estates of the Holy Roman Empire, vindicated the Gospel against sacerdotal encroachment 347 years ago, has just witnessed the inauguration of a monument to his honour. From other statues previously erected to him the new one is distinguished in more than one respect. It is a tribute paid by all Protestant Germany, subscriptions having come in from every county in which the reformed faith has gained a footing. It is a memorial dedicated, not to a man, but to a period, perpetuating alike the effigy of Luther and his associates in the sacred exploit. And it has been unveiled at a time when there are noticeable symptoms of another religious movement, which, whatever its immediate result, will ultimately exercise considerable influence on the destinies of Luther's country and countrymen. In size and rich variety of design the monument has no equal. An improvement even upon Rauch's Frederick the Great, with its host of generals ranged round the base, it is not a statue, but a combination of eleven statues grouped around and surmounted by the gigantic likeness of the Thuringian miner's son. Ascending a few steps, you tread on a granite base, forty feet square, enclosed on the three other sides by a battlemented balustrade. In its centre Luther stands pre-eminent. He is surrounded by congenial minds. Seated on the four pillars projecting from the corners of Luther's pedestal you see, clustering about the master-mind, his four precursors, who attempted what he accomplished. To this noble array the English, French, Italian, and Slave nations have each furnished a member — John Wickliffe, Petrus Waldus, Jeronimo Savonarola, and Jan Huss. Then, turning to the circumference, you notice seven more statues distributed around. Occupying the four corners of the balustrade, and separated from the centre group by the inner space, are the venerable figures of two regal and two clerical allies of the reformatory hero. Frederick the Wise, Elector of Saxony, and Philip the Generous, Landgrave of Hesse, impersonating power and prudence, watch the front; Philip Melanchthon and John Reuchlin, with their solid erudition, are in their rear. To these four, or, including those in the centre group, nine great men—images of real beings—are, with questionable taste, united the symbolical statues of three cities, celebrated in the history of the time, Augsburg, Magdeburg, and Spires. The three majestic women representing them take up the centre of each side of the balustrade. Seated, and looking up to Luther, they, as far as the mere artistic effect is concerned, pleasingly relieve the four corner statues, which are standing and have their faces turned in the same direction as the central figure. To do justice to the many other places which have likewise deserved well of the cause of religious liberty, the battlements of the enclosure are on the inner side decorated with the escutcheons of twenty-four German cities — Brunswick, Bremen, Constance, Eisenach, Eisleben, Emden, Erfurt, Frankfort, Halle, Hamburg, Heilbronn, Jena, Konigsberg, Leipsic, Lindau, Lubeck, Harburg, Memlingen, Nordlingen, Riga, Schmalkalden, Strasburg, Wittenberg, and Worms. Thus stands the wonderful structure before us, a petrified piece of history, silent, yet eloquent to anyone who knows what has once agitated mankind, and has a presentiment of what will agitate them again.

After this general survey, let us examine the details.

On a syenite pedestal of subdued colour, surmounted with two bronze squares, stands Luther. It is the stout, sturdy shape familiar to every eye. It is the dear, old well-known form, with its honest features, and calm, imperturbable eye, as painted by Cranach. With face turned upwards, he rests his clenched fist on the closed Bible, as if uttering the famous verse of his beautiful chorale,—" Das Wort sie sollen lassen stahn." From an artistic point of view it might, perhaps, have been better to give his head a more inclined position, as in a statue of ten and a half feet in height, on a pedestal of sixteen feet, a face lifted up to heaven cannot be well seen from below. A better view, however, is obtained from the side than from the front. Before passing on to the other worthies, we will cast a glance at the pedestal itself. In suggestive detail it is in keeping with the general design. A square of cast bronze, placed on a block of solid stone, supports a similar slab of less dimensions, decorated with inscriptions and reliefs. On its front, a fitting motto of the monument, appear the closing words of Luther's celebrated speech in the Worms Diet :—" Here I stand, I cannot speak nor act otherwise. So help me God. Amen." Under the legend are the medallions of John the Constant and his son

John Frederick of Saxony, who so steadfastly stood by Luther in his troubles. On the opposite side is engraved a passage from another speech of the fiery Reformer :—" The Gospel which the Lord put into the mouth of the Apostles is His sword. With it He strikes the world as with a thunder-bolt." Underneath are the portraits of Ulrich von Hutten and Franz von Sickingen, the two noble knights who brought the chivalrous spirit of their class to the defence of Truth, and its less warlike champions in gown and cowl. To the right of Luther we read the following sentence from his correspondence :—" Faith is life in God, but it is only through the Spirit of Christ that we can hope to understand Holy Writ." Portraits of John Buggenhagen, the Pomeranian Reformer, and Justus Jonas, the intimate friend of Luther, into whose ear, a moment before his death, he poured the confession of his unshaken faith, are inserted on the same side. Finally, on the left we read :—" Those that rightly understand Christ will not be moved by what man may enjoin. They are free, not in the flesh, but in the spirit." John Calvin and Ulrich Zwingli, the founders of the Reformed Church in Switzerland, are aptly placed under this motto, their deviations from Luther proceeding from their partiality to the spirit rather than to the letter of the Bible. The lower slab contains scenes from Luther's life, in alto relievo. Here we have him making his speech in the Worms Parliament, nailing his theses to the door of Wittenberg Cathedral, marrying his Catharine, and translating the Bible in the sequestered castle of Wartburg. For character and finish these smaller castings are greatly praised.

The four figures sitting at the feet of their more successful brother-in-arms next claim our attention. Petrus Waldus, of whom no portrait has been preserved, is represented as a poor wanderer, with torn cloak and staff, and preaching, with the Bible before him, as his guileless heart dictates. Wickliffe, whose features are likewise unknown to posterity, is arrayed in a doctor's garb, a venerable sage, gently stroking his beard, as a man wrapt in contemplation. Huss is the martyr preparing for death. Weighed down with bodily weakness and prolonged imprisonment, he sits, a harrowing picture of misery. But his sharp and emaciated features are lit up by an inspired look, directed towards the crucifix clasped in his hands. The vehement apostle is displayed in the person of Savonarola. He lifts his right hand to Heaven, and beats his heart with his left, looking down on the spectator from under his cowl with eyes flashing fire. To the victorious tranquillity of Luther, these sorrow-laden harbingers of a better day form a contrast, alike beautiful from an artistic, as it is satisfactory from an intellectual point of view.

Of those on the balustrade, Frederick the Wise first meets our eye. Wearing the ermine robe of his Electoral rank, he spurns the imperial crown at his feet. He looks neither to the right nor to the left, but, as was his wont in life, straight forward. His firm, yet unpretending countenance, is characteristic of him who would rather remain ruler of his own hereditary Saxony than sway a vast empire with its opposing factions and interminable discords. Next to Providence, it is to this great and good man that Germany is indebted for the triumph of religious liberty. It was he who protected Luther from the sword and poniard of his enemies, gave him a livelihood, and afforded him leisure for his spiritual work. It was he who concealed him at Wartburg, made him a professor in the theological faculty of Wittenberg, and furnished the wherewithal to maintain that delightful home presided over by Kate. An Englishman must be gratified to reflect, that Frederick the Wise, the most celebrated ancestor of the Prince Consort, stands in a similar relation to the future kings of Great Britain. Unfortunately, the principal branch of his issue have relapsed into Catholicism. In the course of the last century, the Dresden dynasty, to be able to ascend the Polish throne, changed their religion. They have long lost the acquisition for which they sacrificed so much, and, residing again on the Elbe, are now the only Catholics in the country they rule. To revert to the monument, Philip of Hesse, who very nearly forfeited his patrimony by taking up the evangelical cause, is one of the best statues. Leaning on his huge sword, he gazes up to heaven, as though awaiting the dawn of a better day. John Reuchlin, in the cloak of a Doctor of Divinity, is a prototype of the German professor of his time. You almost believe you hear him lecturing, so grave and scholastic is his mien. What he achieved for the Hebrew grammar, Melanchthon, who stands opposite, did for the Greek. Without the aid of these two, Luther's translation of the Bible would have been impossible. The mild expression of countenance and temperate dignity of demeanour which distinguished Melanchthon are well rendered in the statue.

The three symbolic figures representing Magdeburg, Spires, and Augsburg are not all equally perfect,

Magdeburg is praised as a most exquisite performance, Spires censured as a sculptural mistake. The former, the victim of Tilly's hordes, sits before us, discomfited, dishevelled, her arms hanging down, her eyes fixed in despair. She has long recovered from her fall, and again become one of the richest, most industrious, and most cultivated cities of Germany, while her Spanish, Croatian, and Hungarian devastators remain much in the same condition they were in when they burnt her. Spires is intended to be uttering a protest against the reactionary edict of Charles V., but the effect is rather marred by the consideration that a mere mortal woman, subject to the ordinary laws of gravity, were she to raise her hands in so violent a manner with crossed legs, would be in instantaneous peril of falling forward. Augsburg, indicative of the peace concluded within its precincts, is a stately personage with a palm branch in her hand.

I refrain from supplying further details, the pen in this pictorial age standing no chance with photograph and stereoscope in objects of so graphic a nature; but a few words on the impression produced by the whole will not be out of place. Grand as the total effect is, the best critics agree in regretting that the artist who devised the work did not live to see it completed. Rietschel, who in 1856 was commissioned to make the model, died a few years ago, when the statues of Luther and Wickliffe alone had been carried out. The rest were modelled from his sketches by Herren Schilling, Doudorf, and Kietz, his three talented assistants. Their achievements are worthy of the studio whence they proceed; but, while acquitting themselves of their task in excellent style, each of the three sculptors seems to have followed the particular bent of his genius rather than co-operate with the others in the production of an artistic whole. The five statues in the centre, indeed, are generally thought to constitute a splendid ensemble; but the seven others, placed much beneath Luther, and divided from him by nearly thirty feet, are described as having the appearance of separate monuments. To connect them with the centre and each other, it is necessary to bind them with the strong thread of historical association; architecturally they are centrifugal rather than centripetal. The circumstance also that the twelve statues are of four different sizes scarcely contributes to impart to the monument that air of composed symmetry indispensable in every composite work of art. Luther is ten and a half feet high; the figures at his feet, seven feet; the corner statues of the balustrade, eight and a half feet, and those of the towns, six feet.

The inauguration was graced by the presence of the King and the Crown Prince of Prussia, the King of Würtemberg, the Grand Dukes of Weimar and Hesse, Prince William of Baden, and other members of the Royal families of Germany. Of ladies, I see only Princess Charles of Hesse, the mother of Prince Louis, mentioned in the reports. The programme included many sermons, and the prolix verbosity of the reverend gentlemen not mending the matter, the ceremony does not in every particular seem to have produced the solemn effect expected. Times have changed since Luther's days. It is the man, not his creed, that is worshipped now-a-days.

The concourse of strangers was immense, some reports speaking of one hundred thousand, and among them many clergymen. That Her Majesty Queen Victoria considerately sent King William a telegram expressing the sympathies of Protestant England will, no doubt, have been re-telegraphed to your shores.

BERLIN, *June* 27, 1868.

CHAPTER XVIII.

THE ŒCUMENICAL COUNCIL.

AUTHENTIC intelligence having been received respecting the intention of the Pope to cause the Œcumenical Council to make him infallible and the Syllabus a law of the Church,* the Bavarian Government, in the summer of 1869, addressed a circular note to the various continental powers, desiring them to caution the Holy See against extreme steps. This request was not, however, acceded to, the cabinets

---

* The Syllabus, originally issued some years ago, is a catalogue of those errors into which the modern world, the Pope says, is particularly apt to fall. In this catalogue are included all the liberal notions of the times—liberty of religion, liberty of the press, liberty of instruction, liberty of historical, philosophical, and scientific research, independence of the secular governments, &c., &c. Together with the Act proclaiming Infallibility the Syllabus aims at making the Pope Lord Paramount of the Universe, and driving back this nineteenth century of ours to the political and intellectual standard of the middle ages. When first published in the form of a pastoral letter, it appeared the gigantic whim of a twelfth century priest, risen from the dead; now that it has been reduced to canons, and is to be enacted as an ecclesiastical statute, it is a challenge addressed to the entire civilisation of the age. A translation of the Syllabus, Canons, and Infallibility Bill is given in the Appendix.

preferring to postpone secular interference until the Council should be assembled, and the truth of the incredible designs attributed to the Pope established beyond the possibility of a doubt. In the meantime, communications were exchanged between the various German governments, which, as a Berlin semi-official paper was instructed to announce at the time, resulted in the agreement, that, in the event of the Pope persisting in his plans, common measures of defence should be adopted by the German States. Towards the end of the summer, when the day fixed for the opening of the Council was drawing near, and all letters from Rome continued to represent the Pope as inflexible, the German bishops assembled at Fulda, to discuss the means of averting the dangers likely to be brought on by the excessive aspirations of their spiritual superior. With the exception of a few, the German bishops were convinced, that to ask their countrymen to believe in the infallibility of a mere mortal like themselves, and abolish all the most important liberal laws which distinguished modern society from the middle ages, would be running the risk of inflicting a severe blow upon the Catholic interest in Germany. To pit Catholicism against culture would, they were afraid, only damage the former. As the result of their deliberations they issued a common address to their diocesans, exhorting them to look forward with the most perfect confidence to the Council, and to be assured that nothing but what was in accordance with the ancient and unchanging doctrine of the Church could be proclaimed by an assembly which had the promise that the Holy Ghost would be always present in their midst. Both at Rome and in Germany the address was understood as implying a warning to the Pope, not to insist upon the ambitious innovations contemplated.

That of all European cabinets, that of Bavaria should have been most disquieted by the extraordinary proceedings of Pio IX., is easily accounted for by the peculiar political situation of the kingdom. If Bavaria has any chance of preserving her present degree of independence and keeping out of a united Germany, as her governmental circles desire, it is by relying upon the Catholic portion of her inhabitants and setting them against the Protestant north. But such a policy will be rendered very difficult if the Pope insist upon hurrying on a rupture between the religion he presides over and the educated and enlightened men of all denominations and countries. In Germany, especially, where freethinkers abound, the Pope is incurring the imminent peril of estranging all the more cultivated strata of society. Should an anti-Papal movement form itself in this country, it will, therefore, shake not only Catholicism in its present form, but also the political parties counting upon it as their principal *raison d'être*. The fear of some such catastrophe occurring in no remote future has had visible effect upon the latest politics of the Bavarian government, as well as upon that portion of its Catholic subjects under the control of the priests. The Bavarian government, while doing all in their power to induce the Pope to desist from his dangerous designs, have, at the same time, thought it necessary to provide against the contingency of their endeavours proving abortive. They have warned and entreated the Pope, yet with an eye to future embarrassments possibly arising from his refusal, been careful to secure a friend in another and this a Protestant quarter. It is well known, that though keeping out of the Northern Confederacy, they have uniformly acknowledged the obligation imposed upon them by the military treaties with Prussia — the obligation, namely, to stand by Prussia in all wars offensive and defensive. By cautioning the Pontiff, they intended to avert the religious troubles, which to them might become a source of political difficulties; by remaining true to the treaties binding them to Prussia in war, but leaving them independent in peace, they wished so to regulate their behaviour as to give their powerful ally no formal ground for absorbing them in the confederacy, in case their domestic religious troubles should seem to facilitate the process. Very different from this discreet conduct was the bearing of the Bavarian Ultramontanes. A relic of the obsolete past in a progressive age and country, they have long had an instinctive propensity for compensating the weakness of their position by strong words and savage action. In the present instance, the fanaticism prevalent at Rome seems to have absolutely deprived them of their senses. Instead of prudently steering their course to avoid the rocks ahead, they are clamouring for a virtual abandonment of those military treaties with Prussia, the preservation of which their more sensible government regards as the principal guarantee of continued political independence. Instead of using their influence with the Pope to induce him to pause in a course likely to ruin him and them, the only effect their fear of coming dangers has upon them is to make them wish for an immediate and complete separation from that Prussia, which, they apprehend, will derive additional strength from the mistakes of their ecclesiastical head. How very small their chance of success, will be seen from what follows. Here suffice it to say, that with nearly all educated Bavarian Catholics opposing the Ultramontanes, the latter mainly depend on the good-will of the peasantry. Nearly one-third of the population of Bavaria are, moreover, Protestants, and as such anything but favourable to Romanists and anti-national tendencies.

CHAPTER XIX.

EPISCOPAL HERETICS.

THE Roman priests employed in preparing the resolutions of the Council have not only rightly interpreted the meaning of the address the German bishops have conjointly issued on this important topic, but are so irritated by the warnings therein administered, that they have actually committed the imprudence of giving vent to their feelings. In the " Civilta Cattolica," the ecclesiastical organ of the Papacy, the German bishops are designated "German heretics." The bishops heretics ! No wonder, then, that those of the German Catholic laity, who, in the interest of Catholicism, recently petitioned the bishops to prevent the most extreme of the announced votes of the Council, should, by the same official paper, be called "rebels." The priests at Rome must look upon this 19th century of ours in a way very different from the usual one, if they think they can afford to treat to such phraseology the only section of the educated classes who, in Germany, still adhere to the Papal doctrine. For it is from this section alone, that the petitions proceed. That the bishops who have this provoking epithet flung in their faces are good Catholics, need not be stated; as to the laity, who also come in for their share of contumely, they have notoriously drawn up those objectionable petitions only because they wish to protect the Church against the follies of some of her leaders, and prevent her becoming a moral impossibility in a civilised and progressive age. To prove the genuineness of their orthodoxy, the petitioners have, moreover, expressly admitted the obligation they are under as Roman Catholics to acknowledge any decrees whatsoever that might be passed at the Council. Was it possible to preface more humbly the prayer which doubted the propriety of making the Pope infallible, and the Syllabus, that repudiation of all modern civilisation, a dogma of the Church? To the Bonn, Coblentz, and Trèves petitions to that effect, another has just been added, addressed to the Bishop of Paderborn. Another sign of the times, which might caution the leading powers at Rome not to overstrain the bow, is the second reply of the Munich theological faculty to the questions put by the Bavarian Government. The first reply was given by the majority of the professors; the second bears the signature of the minority—consisting of two professors only,—who found it impossible to agree with their theological brethren. The first, while gently dissuading the Pope from proclaiming the Syllabus and his own infallibility as a dogma, yet asserted it to be the duty of Catholic Christians to believe those dogmas should they happen to be proclaimed; the second, not content with this feeble manifestation, boldly declares that the enactment of Syllabus and infallibility would neither change the existing relations between Church and State, nor oblige Roman Catholics to believe that God has appointed the Pope to be the Sovereign of all Sovereigns, or exempted the clergy from all supervision of the secular authorities. Unless the Roman dignitaries are convinced that no crisis can ever injure *them*, they will do well to notice these pregnant symptoms.

BERLIN, *September* 22, 1869.

CHAPTER XX.

THE GERMAN BISHOPS AND THE ŒCUMENICAL COUNCIL.

The opposition of the German and Austrian bishops at the Council to the Infallibility party is viewed with rather mixed feelings in the country they come from: from their antecedents these dignitaries are many of them known as enemies of modern enlightenment, advocates of the Syllabus and determined supporters of such a re-arrangement of Germany, as shall destroy the nation as a whole, enfeeble Protestant Prussia, and restore the ascendancy of the Catholic House of Hapsburg. If they are now playing a liberal part at the Council, one, and this a rather popular explanation for this strange metamorphosis, is, to assume them to believe, that by sanctioning the new enormities claimed by the Pope, they will, in so rationalistic a country as Germany, dig away the soil, on which to exercise their reactionary practices in the future. Infallibility is supposed to be regarded by them as too strong a dose for this susceptible age and nation: it will be believed in by but few, and may cause many to consider the Church as incompatible with civilization. People, of course, do not deny, that some of the bishops, in their resistance to the contemplated dogma, are actuated by more conscientious motives, while others may be naturally anxious to retain their ancient share of influence in the Church, which would be annihilated by rendering the Pope omnipotent. But from a broader point of view, the majority of these recusant ecclesiastics, in their opposition to the Pope, are thought to be partisans of reaction, not of progress. Their declaring against Infallibility, public opinion accounts for by crediting them with no more elevated motives than can be derived from a conviction, that the thing is too extravagant to be made palatable to their diocesans. These suspicions have been lately strengthened by the wording of the Anti-Infallibility address presented to the Council by a number of bishops, and drawn up by Cardinal Rauscher of Vienna. This address, the work of a notorious Ultramontane, and signed by many equally famous with himself for their ardent devotion to the Holy See, frankly declares it inopportune in so latitudinarian an age to exact of the people "heavier obligations" in the matter of faith than were imposed by the Council of Trent. The text of this remarkable document runs as follows:—

"Most Holy Father,—We have received the draught of a petition circulating among the Fathers of the Œcumenical Council, and calling upon them to declare supreme and infallible authority to be vested in the Roman Pontifex when imparting apostolical teaching to all the faithful upon subjects connected with religion and morals. It is certainly strange that the judges of matters religious should be asked to decide a question before it has been discussed, but as thou, most Holy Father, divinely appointed to tend the flock of Christ, so piously takest care of the souls redeemed by His blood, and with paternal compassion lookest upon the dangers threatening them, we have thought it right to address ourselves to thee in this matter. The times are past when the Catholics used to contest the rights of the Holy See. We all are aware that as the human body, without the head, is but a mutilated trunk, so can no Council of the entire Church be held without the successor of St. Peter; and we all obey the mandates of the Holy See with ready willingness. As regards the authority which the faithful are obliged to concede to the Roman Pontiff, this has been settled by the Council of Trent,

The Bishops and the Œcumenical Council. 181

and also by the Council of Florence. The decrees of the latter, particularly, ought to be the more faithfully observed, inasmuch as, having been enacted with the common consent of Latins and Greeks, they are destined some day, when the Lord will take pity on the Orient, now oppressed by so many evils, to become the basis of the re-union of the Church. Nor must we leave it unmentioned that at a time when the Church is compelled more earnestly than ever to wage war against those who denounce religion as a mere fiction, vain and idle indeed, yet pernicious to the human race, it cannot be opportune to exact of the Catholic nations, already exposed to so much seduction and temptation, heavier duties (*majora*) than were enjoined on them by the Council of Trent. It is true that, although Bellarminus, and with him the whole Catholic Church, affirms that matters of faith are to be chiefly decided by Apostolical tradition and the common consent of the Church, and although the best way to ascertain the decision of the Church is to convene a Universal Synod, yet from the Council of the Apostles and Elders of Jerusalem down to the Council of Nice have the innumerable errors of the local Churches been checked and extinguished by the decisions of the successors of St. Peter, approved by the entire Church. Nor do we deny that while all faithful believers are bound to obey the behests of the Holy See, there are pious and erudite men teaching over and above this that any utterances of the Supreme Pontiff on matters of religion and morality, when formally (*ex cathedrâ*) made and announced, must be held irrefragable, albeit lacking the express consent of the Church. Yet we must not omit stating that grave objections to this teaching may be based on the acts and utterances of the Fathers of the Church, —objections supported by the evidence of genuine historical documents and the Catholic doctrine itself. Unless the difficulties arising from this circumstance are entirely solved and done away with, it is possible that the doctrine advocated in the above-mentioned petition will some day be inculcated on the Christian people as one revealed by the Almighty. We have no wish to dwell upon this prospect (*verum ab hisce discutiendis refugit animus*), and confidently entreat thee to obviate the necessity of such a discussion. We think we may say that performing episcopal functions among the more eminent nations of the Catholic world, and being by daily experience well conversant with the state of things in our respective countries, the enactment of the doctrine proposed will only supply fresh arms of attack to the enemies of religion, and enable them to rouse invidious feelings even in better and more virtuous men (*melioris notæ viros*) than themselves. We are certain, moreover, that such an event in one part of Europe, at any rate, would be taken advantage of by the Governments to infringe the remnant of rights still possessed by the Church. Having laid this before thy Holiness with the sincerity due to the common father of all true believers, we beseech thee to prohibit the discussion in the Œcumenical Council of the doctrine recommended in the above-mentioned petition. Prostrating ourselves at thy feet, both in our own name and on behalf of the nations which we have undertaken to guide to the knowledge of God (*ad Deum perducendos*), we ask for thy apostolical blessing. We remain the most humble, most obedient, and devoted servants of thy Holiness."

The signatures affixed to this address are still unknown.

I append the protest of the German and Austrian Bishops against the rules and regulations of the Œcumenical Council, devised, it is well known, with a view to muzzle opponents.

"Most Holy Father,—All the Bishops of the entire

world, and among them we the undersigned, most ardently desire that the Œcumenical Council, so happily inaugurated under the auspices of your Holiness, may be successfully continued, so that it may supply the various nations with remedies against the many new evils oppressing them, and impart to the Holy Church of God fresh means and strength to fulfil the mission divinely imposed upon it. In order that this object may be the more surely attained, we take the liberty of acquainting your Holiness with the anxiety we feel concerning a matter connected with the debates of this ecclesiastical assembly. In taking this step we are animated by that devotion to the Holy Apostolical See always felt by the Bishops of the entire world, and never more so than at this present time.

"In the rules and regulations of the Council prescribed by your Holiness the most important clause, perhaps, is the second, referring to the privilege of the members to direct the attention of the assembly to such matters as they may think fit to introduce. There are those who think that by the clause in question the right of the assembled Fathers to start any discussion they may deem conducive to the public weal has been taken away, its exercise having been made dependent on a favour to be only exceptionally accorded. Most Holy Father, we are all firmly convinced, that the body of the Church cannot be strong and healthy unless possessed of a lofty and powerful head, and that the proceedings of the Synod cannot be correct and orderly unless the divine rights of the Primacy are properly protected and observed. But if this is undoubtedly true, it is not less so that the other members of the mystical body of Christ likewise require to be protected in their special functions, and that the College of Bishops, more particularly, must be in a position to exercise the rights inherent to them by virtue of their office and character, if the head is to retain its proper strength and to act safely and undisturbedly. By God's ordinance the head and the body are intimately connected and inseparably united with each other. Equally as, therefore, in the exercise of your Holiness's undoubted privilege, your Holiness has condescended to lay down the manner of procedure in the Holy Synod, and prescribe the wisest and most effective rules concerning the manner and order of treatment of the subjects introduced, so the Fathers of the Council, if feeling prompted to prefer aught connected with the welfare of the Church, or to make a proposition aiming at the furtherance of the same, have always justly enjoyed the right to do so by virtue of their position and office, the only condition exacted being that they should speak with the devotion and veneration due to the Head of the Church. We state this the more confidently, inasmuch as your Holiness has yourself condescended to exhort us to express freely whatever we may consider to be calculated to promote the public weal; and inasmuch as, in taking this step, we are only following in the footsteps of the most celebrated and most sacred Council of Trent (Sess. XXIV., cap. 21).

"In our opinion, therefore, there can have been no intention to infringe our rights by the above-mentioned clause; and we should be greatly strengthened in this our conviction if your Holiness would kindly permit that the committee appointed for the preliminary examination of propositions introduced by members be reinforced by some Fathers elected by the Council out of their own midst, and also that members introducing propositions be allowed access to the said committee, to enable them to take part in the examination thereof.

"In submitting this, with filial devotion, to your wise consideration and judgment, we hope, Most Holy Father, that what, animated by the purest intentions, we have been prompted to prefer will be well received.

"Prostrating ourselves at the feet of your Holiness, we are, the most obedient servants of your Holiness,

> "Cardinal SCHWARZENBERG.
> " FÜRSTENBERG, Archbishop of Olmutz.
> " GREGOR SCHERR, Archbishop of Munich.
> " MICHAEL VON DEINLEIN, Archbishop of Bamberg.
> " LUDWIG HAYNALD, Archbishop of Kolosa.
> " HEINRICH FÖRSTER, Archbishop of Breslau.
> " PANCRATIUS DINKEL, Bishop of Angsburg.
> " VALENTIN VIERY, Bishop of Görz.
> " GREGOR SIMONOVICZ, Archbishop of Lemberg (of the Armenian Rite).
> " BARTHOLOMAEUS, Bishop of Trieste.
> " JOANNES ZIRZIK, Bishop of Budweis.
> " GEORG DOBRILA, Episcop. Parent.
> " JACOBUS STEPNISNIGG, Episcop. Lavantin.
> " ALEXANDER BONNAZ, Bishop of Csanad.
> " MATTHAEUS EBERHARD, Bishop of Trier.
> " EDUARD JACOB, Bishop of Hildesheim.
> " MICHAEL FOGARASSY, Bishop of Transylvania.
> " JOSEPH STROSSMAYER, Bishop of Bosnia and Syrmia (Austrian Croatia).
> " STEPHAN LIPOVNICZKY, Bishop of Grosswardein.
> " SIGISMUND KOVACS, Bishop of Fünfkirchen.
> " LUDWIG FERWERK, Bishop of Leontopolis.
> " JOANNES BECKMANN, Bishop of Osnabrück.
> " GEORG SMICIKLAS, Episcop. Crisiens.
> " HIERONYMUS ZEIDLER, Abbas Strahoviensis (Prague).
> " WILHELM KETTELER, Bishop of Mayence.
> " PETRUS KENRICK, Archbishop of St. Louis, United States."

It may not be superfluous to add, that the above translations have been made from the Latin originals.

Berlin, *January* 23, 1870.

CHAPTER XXI.

GERMAN OBJECTIONS TO INFALLIBILITY AS ADVOCATED BY THE SPANISH, ITALIAN, AND ORIENTAL BISHOPS.

DR. DÖLLINGER, the learned Roman Catholic professor and prelate at Munich, to whom we are indebted for the famous treatise entitled "Janus," once more takes up the cudgels against the Jesuits, and in the *Allgemeine Zeitung* publishes the following article on the address of the Spanish and Italian bishops in favour of Infallibility:—

"We have just read the remarkable address presented by certain members of the Œcumenical Council to the Pope requesting His Holiness to cause his own infallibility to be declared a dogma by the ecclesiastical assembly now sitting. The bishops whose names appear in the address actually demand that 180,000,000 of people shall, under threats of excommunication and eternal perdition, be forced in future to believe and profess what the Church has hitherto neither believed nor taught. Even those who have till now supposed Papal infallibility a reality could not believe in it—that is to say, not in the sense properly belonging to this word in the Christian acceptation of the term. There is an immense difference between belief (*fides divina*) and the mere adoption by the reasoning faculties of a probable hypothesis. The Catholic is only permitted to believe that which has been imparted and prescribed to him by the Church itself, as Divinely revealed, indispensable, and incontrovertible truth. He may believe only that, the denial of which would exclude him from the Church, and the reverse of which is absolutely prohibited and rejected as heresy by the Church. Accordingly, no man from the first ages of the Church to this day has believed in the infallibility of the Pope—*i.e.*, has so believed in it as he believes in God, Christ, the Trinity, &c.; the utmost that can be conceded being that many have assumed it to be probable and in keeping with the laws of the human understanding (*fides humana*), that the Pope has this particular prerogative. The alteration, then, in the belief and doctrine of the Church which the bishops joining in the address wish to see carried through, would be an event without precedent in the history of the Church—an event the like of which has not occurred in eighteen centuries. They are asking for an ecclesiastical revolution, which is to change the entire basis of our religious belief, clothing a single individual, the Pope, with the powers hitherto wielded by the entire Church, which is eternal and ubiquitous. Up to the present day the Catholic has been wont to say, 'I believe, in this or that doctrine on the testimony of the entire Church of all ages because that Church has the promise of existing for ever, and for ever remaining in the possession of the truth.' But in future a Roman Catholic would have to reason thus : 'I believe, because the Pope, having been declared infallible, has commanded this doctrine to be taught and believed. As to his infallibility, I believe it because he asserts it of himself.' For although four hundred or six hundred bishops, assembled at Rome in 1870, may pronounce the Pope to be infallible, any resolution taken by them derives force only from its having been sanctioned by the Pope. The Council without the Pope being fallible, it is the Pope whose consent renders the resolutions of the Council valid. And thus everything resolves itself into the Pope testifying to his own qualities, which, it must be confessed, is a remarkably simple mode of reasoning. Who, when witnessing this, can help remembering what a far higher being said 1840 years ago?—' If I bear witness of Myself, my witness is not true.' John 5, 31."

Other objections to the address may be briefly stated thus :—

" 1. It confines the infallibility of the Pope to those utterances and decrees issued by him to all believers, for the instruction of the whole Catholic Church. Hence it must be inferred that whenever Popes have formerly addressed single persons, corporate bodies, or particular churches, they were liable to fall into error. Now, it is a striking fact that during the first twelve or thirteen centuries of the Church all utterances of the Pope on questions of doctrine, were addressed either to single individuals, the bishop of a single country, &c. In the thousand years that the Oriental Church has been united to that of Rome it has never received a Papal decree addressed to all its bishops at once; only individual patriarchs or Emperors have been distinguished by receiving letters from the Pope connected with matters of belief. Hence it follows that for a thousand years the Popes have themselves been unaware of the condition indispensably required to stamp their utterances with infallibility—viz., that those utterances must be directed to the Church as a whole. In point of fact, the assumption of this requisite is only three hundred years prior to the present date. In 1562 Johann Hessels, professor of theology at Löwen (Louvain), in Flanders, was the first to start this doctrine. From him it was borrowed by Bellarmin, who supported it by citations from the false decretals of Isidorus, and the forged testimony of St. Cyril. It is these men who first asked the world to believe that the Popes, although by merely changing the superscription of their epistles they might have secured for themselves that highest prerogative of infallibility, yet unaccountably abstained from doing so, thus exposing the addressees to the risk of being led into error by observing injunctions given without the guarantee of Divine Truth.

"2. The assertion of the address that, in accordance with the constant and universal tradition of the Church, Papal decisions on matters of faith are unalterable, is untrue. The reverse is the case. The Church has always tested the letters of the Popes on matters of faith, and, according to the result of this examination, either approved them, as the Council of Chalcedon did the letter of Leo, or rejected them as erroneous, as the fifth Council (553) did the constitution of Vigilius, and the sixth Council (681) the epistle of Honorius.

"3. It is not true that at the second Council of Lyons (1274) a decree was adopted with the consent of the Greeks and the Latins, enacting that disputes on matters of faith must be decided by the Popes. Neither the Greeks nor the Latins—*i.e.*, the occidental bishops assembled at Lyons—voted that decree, but the Emperor Michael Palæologus having had its adoption made a condition of his readmission to the Church by Pope Clement IV., and finding his power severely menaced by the Emperor Baldwin and King Charles of Sicily, submitted to the terms ecclesiastically imposed on him, and, notwithstanding the prolonged resistance of the Greek bishops and nation, bowed to the Papal demand. The letter in which he inserted a passage to this effect was read at the Council, and confirmed by his representative, the Logothetes. But shortly afterwards he, in his own capital of Constantinople, declared the three concessions made to the Pope illusory. (*Pachymeres* de Michaele Palæologo, 5, 22.) With regard to the bishops assembled at the Council, they never were in a position to discuss, or, indeed, give any opinion on the dogmatic passage imposed upon the Emperor.

"4. A garbled version of the decree of the Florentine Synod is given in the Address, the principal passage, the wording of which could be accomplished only after long negotiations between the Greeks and Italians, being simply omitted. This passage, so very important, because qualifying all that preceded, is as follows:—" Juxta cum modum qui et in gestis et in sacris canonibus oecumenicorum conciliorum continetur.' (Anglice—'The power of the Pope is to be wielded according to the deliberations and canons of the Œcumenical Council.') The Pope and the Cardinals, it is well known, insisted that the primacy of the Pope should be declared as exercised 'juxta dicta Sanctorum' (according to the testimony of the Saints). But the Greeks opposed this enactment, being well aware that in 'the testimony of the Saints' was a large amount of spurious or falsified utterances. Had not, in the seventh sitting of the Council, the Latin Archbishop Andrea gone the length of appealing to the evidence of the spurious writings of Saint Cyril, which, ever since Thomas de Aquino and Pope Urban IV. allowed themselves to be deceived by them, were regarded as authoritative in the Occident, but rejected by the Greeks? The Emperor on this occasion expressly observed, that if one of the good fathers in a letter to the Pope had perhaps expressed himself in language of complimentary devotion, it would be unfair for the addressee to claim any rights and privileges on such ground. After much discussion the Latins yielded, the 'dicta Sanctorum' disappeared from the draught, and the deliberations of the Œcumenical Councils and sacred Canons were adopted as the measure of the power to be wielded by the Papacy. By this resolution Papal Infallibility was absolutely excluded, as there is nothing in the ancient Councils and the pre-Isidoric Canons, common to both churches, which establishes such a prerogative. On the contrary, the whole ancient legislation of the Church, as well as the proceedings of the seven Œcumenical Councils, are evidently based on the supposition that the highest doctrinal authority is vested in the entire Church, but not in one alone of the five Patriarchs (for this, and no more, was the Pope in the eyes of the Greeks). Archbishop Bessarion, moreover, in the name of all Greeks declared at the Council that the Pope was inferior to the Council, or, what is the same, that he was not infallible. (Sess. IX. Concil. Labbei XIII., 150.) It is consequently a mutilation, tantamount to a falsification, if the Bishops in quoting the decree of the Florentine Synod in their address, omit the principal sentence, on which was laid the greatest stress by those for whom the decree was drawn up.

In the eyes of the Greeks this sentence was so indispensable that they declared they would leave the Council and return home unless it were inserted. They also insisted, and with the like success, that all the rights and privileges of the other Patriarchs were expressly guaranteed to them in the decree. As to the Patriarchs having the right of assisting in the definition and enactment of the doctrine, this the Popes had themselves formerly accorded.

"There is another reason for the mutilation of the Florentine decree, perpetrated by the author of the Address. He may have asked himself whether he was to give the Latin text in its original form, corresponding to the Greek, and quoted by Flavius Blondus, secretary of Pope Eugen IV. and the older theologians—'Quemadmodum et in actis Conciliorum et in sacris canonibus continetur.' (Anglice—'As the power of the Pope is defined in the deliberations and sacred canons of the Council.') Or was he to endorse the falsification first committed by Abraham Bartholomæus, replacing the 'et' by 'etiam?' By this 'etiam' (meaning 'also,' and therefore implying that the Papal power had been confirmed even by the Councils), the sense of the decree is perfectly changed, and the object of the passage in question entirely subverted.

But, notwithstanding this, and the manifest forgery committed, this 'etiam' has been copied by the editors of the proceedings of the Councils, as also by the authors of dogmatic text-books. It is high time to remove this stone of stumbling to the Orientals, and restore the genuine text in accordance with the Greek original. It is true that after this amendment the decree will be no longer capable of being turned to account by the Infallibilists, as was incontrovertibly proved, as much as two hundred years ago, by D. Marca, Archbishop of Paris (Concord. Sacerd. et Imperii, 3, 8), who observes very pertinently:—
'Verba Graeca in sincero sensu accepta modum exercitio potestatis pontificae imponunt ei similem quem ecclesia Gallicana tuetur. At e contextus Latini depravata lectione eruitur plenam esse Papae potestatem, idque probari actis Conciliorum et Canonibus.' (Anglice—'Taken in their true sense the Greek words restrain the exercise of the Pontifical power in the same manner as is done by the Gallican Church. But the corrupt Latin version attributes unlimited power to the Pope, and refers to the proceedings and canons of the Councils in proof of this.')

"The Address indignantly declares against those who doubt the Œcumenical character of the Florentine

Synod ('Acerbissimi Catholicæ doctrinæ impugnatores . . blaterare non erubescunt;' *Anglice*—'Those worst enemies of the Catholic faith that do not blush to repeat the absurd story,' &c.) But let facts speak for themselves. On the Council of Basle resolving upon sundry reforms unpalatable to Rome the Florentine Synod was convened to do away with those objectionable decrees. Opened at Ferrara April 9, 1438, its proceedings had to be put off for six months, so small was the number of Bishops present. From all Northern Europe, then entirely Catholic, from Germany, the Scandinavian countries, Poland, Bohemia, France, Castile, Portugal, not a single Bishop had appeared. Nine-tenths of the then Catholic world took no part in the meeting on principle, because they thought it an assembly illegally acting as a rival to the Basle Council, and because all men foresaw that nothing in the way of a reform of the Church, urgent as it was, would be attempted at Florence. With much ado Pope Eugen at last managed to collect about fifty Italian Bishops, subsequently swelled by a few ecclesiastics sent by the Duke of Burgundy, and a sprinkling of Provençals and Spaniards. Altogether only sixty-two Bishops signed the decree. The Greek prelates with their Emperor had in the hour of sorest need been attracted by promises of money, ships, and soldiers, the Pope, moreover, engaging to defray their expenses in Ferrara and Florence, and also pay for their journey home. On showing themselves refractory the Pope withdrew provisions, so that, compelled by the Emperor and hunger, they eventually affixed their signatures to papers which, subsequently, nearly all revoked. The judgment passed on this episode by a Greek contemporary writer, Amyrutius, which is quoted by the Roman scholar, Leo Allatius (de perp. consens., 3, 1, 4), is a fair reflex of Greek public opinion in those days. 'Is there any one,' asks Amyrutius, 'that can seriously denominate this Synod an Œcumenical one, which paid cash down for articles of faith, and which openly indulging in Simonistic practices carried its resolutions by promising pecuniary and military help to those that enacted them?' In France previous to the Revolution the Florentine Synod was regarded as spurious, and Cardinal Guise declared as much at the Council of Trent without being contradicted. The Portuguese theologian, Payva de Andrada, says on this head, 'Florentinam Synodum sola Gallia. . . . pro Œcumenica nunquam habuit, quippe quam neque adire dum agitaretur, neque admittere jam perfectam atque absolutam voluerit.'

Anglice—'France alone never acknowledged the Florentine Synod as Œcumenical, declining to take part in it, while sitting, and to ratify its proceedings when over.'—(Defens. fid. Trident. p. 431, ed. Colon. 1580). The rest of the Address endeavours to show that the enactment of the new article of faith is most opportune just now, and even urgently required, because some persons calling themselves Catholics have recently disputed the alleged infallibility of the Pope. Of itself, the Address gives us to understand, it would not have been absolutely necessary to augment the doctrinal canon by a new article of faith, but things had assumed an aspect rendering such a step unavoidable. It is well known that for several years past the Order of Jesuits, supported by others of a like way of thinking, has kept up an agitation in Italy, France, Germany, and England, canvassing for the dogma that is to be. A special religious society has been established and publicly announced by the Jesuits, having for its object to pray and act in behalf of the new dogma. The "Civiltà," the principal organ of the Jesuits published at Rome, has announced it as the main task of the Council to present the expectant world with the one article of faith still wanting; and their "Laacher Stimmen" and Vienna publications have discussed the same theme diffusely, and with unwearied repetition. The Jesuits contend that it is the duty of all of opposite notions to remain passive spectators of their doings, and abstain from examining into the consistency of the arguments preferred in their numerous printed utterances. Unfortunately, however, their expectations have not been fulfilled; some men have had the unprecedented hardihood to break through the holy silence exacted, and announce a different opinion. Of course, such an offence can only be made up for by augmenting the articles of faith and changing the catechisms and all books on the Catholic religion."

Dr. Döllinger, the author of this article, whose sincere belief in the doctrines of his Church has never been impugned, is a prelate and one of the most learned Catholic professors of theology in Germany. In his opposition to the majority in the Council he is supported by nearly every educated co-religionist in the land, even the strictest among them foreseeing that to render their creed less intelligible will only serve to make it less acceptable. But a few weeks ago the King of Bavaria, the only Catholic Sovereign of Germany (as the King of Saxony, although likewise a Catholic, cannot politically be so regarded, his subjects being

Protestant), addressed a letter to Dr. Döllinger in which he strongly approved his theological labours.*

A very different letter on the Council has just been addressed to the Cracow *Czas* by the Rev. X. Sosnovski, provisionally intrusted with the administration of the diocese of Lublin. M. Sosnovski, the only priest present at the Council from Russian Poland, a short time ago secretly absented himself from his diocese, and in disguise crossed the frontier on his way to Rome. Whether he did so from an ardent desire to attend the Church assembly, or whether he had reason to fear that the Russians were going to send him to Siberia, as has been done with nearly all his colleagues in their dominion, does not appear. Rejoicing in his escape, and much pleased to have near him one at least of high ecclesiastical rank from so religious a country, the Pope, though M. Sosnovski is not yet ordained as Bishop, as an exceptional favour admitted him to the Council. But

---

* The publication in the *Allgemeine Zeitung* of the above article has since been rewarded by the Burgomasters and Town Council of Munich conferring upon Dr. Döllinger the freedom of their city. Munich is the only Catholic capital of Germany. The King of Bavaria has availed himself of the recurrence of Döllinger's birthday, to congratulate him on his manly vindication of the truth. Nearly all the most eminent professors of Catholic theology in Germany have signified their assent to his opinions.

this distinction seems to have been too great to be credited by the right rev. officials standing sentinel at the doors of St. Peter. In his letter to the *Czas* M. Sosnovski describes at length how he had to fight for admittance into the Chapel, and how even when he got in, at the last moment of walking up to His Holiness to take the oath, somebody caught hold of his sleeve and pulled him back. However, the gallant Pole shook himself free, and, striding manfully forward, ultimately reached the Papal Throne. On recognizing him, Pio Nono, as the object of his favour relates with grateful emotion, condescended to interrupt the solemnity of the sacred act by uttering the following words in Italian :—" Ecco il mio Polacco. Sta bene." All Polish papers reproduce the story which brings to them the greeting of their sole protector.

BERLIN, *January* 22, 1870.

CHAPTER XXII.

MORE GERMAN OBJECTIONS TO INFALLIBILITY.

ON the subject of infallibility it is becoming more and more evident that all German Sovereigns and many German Bishops are arrayed against the Pope. Not to speak of conscientious scruples, the Bishops are obviously afraid that to declare the Pope a god will outrage the feelings of every civilized being among their flocks, and cause many hitherto accommodating, though, perhaps, somewhat indifferent, members of the Church to desert, renounce, and attack it. As to the Sovereigns, they have no wish to assist the Pope in arousing a religious movement which might go any length, and which, should it attain serious proportions, would be sure to extend to Protestantism also. In Germany religious apathy—the prevailing feature of the age—is accompanied with so much downright opposition to all that has been hitherto considered orthodox that for the Pope to treat this country on a footing of intellectual equality with Italy, Spain, and France, and desire the Germans to adore and idolize him in the same way he asks others, is to let off squibs over a barrel of gunpowder. They need not necessarily ignite the inflammable material over which they fly and crack, but they may do so. Already Protestant liberalism is preparing for such an event. You remember the assault on the monastery at Moabit, and the discussion to which the opening ceremony of this new establishment, marked by its provoking character, gave rise in the summer. In consequence numerous petitions have since been addressed to the Prussian Parliament, some requesting that the law be changed so as to prevent the indefinite multiplication of convents, others insisting that the present law, rigorously carried out, would enable Government to prohibit the monks from taking charge of schools, orphanages, and other charitable institutions. Without special inducement to the contrary, these petitions would have given rise to an animated debate, and united Protestants and Rationalists in the House in repelling the accusations so noisily brought against them in these latter days by Rome. Such a special motive for caution seems, however, to have arisen, and it is no other than the fear that by making what might be interpreted as a Protestant move—not against an extreme party in the

Catholic Church, but against all Catholics,— they might interfere with the split now going on in the bosom of the Papal Establishment. This view being shared also by liberal Catholics, there is little doubt that Parliament will resolve for the present to hold its tongue on the delicate subject of monasteries, and quietly pass over all irate petitions to the order of the day.

In the meantime, two more Catholic professors of theology have publicly declared against Infallibility. Professor Michelis, of the Clerical Seminary of Braunsberg, in East Prussia, writes the following vigorous letter, dated January 21, to the editor of the *Allgemeine Zeitung* :—

" Permit me, in a few words, to characterize the address drawn up in favour of infallibility. It is not a dogmatic, but a diplomatic document. It not only avoids making use of the term 'infallibility,' but also omits alluding to the preliminary question whether the Bishops are an integral portion of the ecclesiastical body appointed to teach the nations of the earth. If they are, how is it possible for the Pope to claim infallibility independent of the Bishops? If they are not, of what weight are their votes? If the Pope is really infallible, he cannot be fallible in declaring himself infallible, and Pius IX., in this nineteenth century of ours, must not then hesitate to announce what Innocent III. in the thirteenth century regarded as heresy. Obviously, from a dread of having thus logically to analyze the matter, the signers of the infallibility address have given it its diplomatic form. It is for this reason that the address, intrinsically untrue from beginning to end, surreptitiously replaces the Primacy and that which belongs to it by the, as yet, undefined notion of infallibility. The address, moreover, is conceived in a passionate spirit, and terribly uncharitable. Not condescending to enter upon the arguments preferred by the opposition, and entirely overlooking that they are based on the belief of the Church and the general acceptation of the Catholic world as it has been so long received, the address merely notices the existence of an opposition to make it a ground for enacting infallibility and all but provoking apostasy. In keeping with these passionate proceedings is the coarseness observable in the wording of the address. We actually find the word *blaterare* ('stupid prattle') used in reference to the highest among the assembled Fathers. Taking all this into account, the address is no more than a party intrigue of the Jesuits, who, having failed to produce a more direct definition of infallibility, have had recourse to this expedient. The adoption of the address by the Council would be a sorry victory of Jesuitic party feelings over the true spirit of the Church, and a calamity to the Church and mankind."

Considering this emanates from a priest professionally engaged in educating other priests, one must say that if the Pope come to grief it is not for want of warning. Opinions similar to these have been avowed by Dr. Schulte, one of the most renowned Professors of Canon Law at the University of Prague. In noticing Maret's *Du Concile Générale et de la Paix Religieuse* in the *Theologisches Literaturblatt*, the best German Catholic review, published at Bonn, he says:—

"It is a fact that the Church never held the Popes to be infallible. Otherwise, how could Popes have been condemned for heresy by Œcumenical Councils? How could these sentences have been regarded as just and valid by other Popes? How could Popes have been deposed, and how could others elected in their stead have been recognized by the Church? How could dogmatic decisions emanating from the Popes have been subjected to the examination of the Councils, and in some cases been withdrawn by their authors?

How could the Church have adhered to the conviction that Popes, for certain derelictions, may be arraigned and even condemned? How could several Popes, as, for instance, Gregory VII., have thought it necessary to free themselves from the suspicion of heresy by oath? All which proves that the Church did not from the beginning believe the Popes to be infallible, and that infallibility was only attributed to the Church as a whole. Whether the Church passed a verdict at a General Council, or whether it merely approved decisions given by Popes, or whether the Pope and episcopacy sanctioned the mandates of local Councils, the concurrence of Pope and Church was always required for an infallible decree. This being the case, we may confidently trust that neither the Council nor the majority of Bishops assembled will take the much dreaded step of raising infallibility to the dignity of a dogma. Infallibility is a quality beyond what belongs to man. Such a quality can be created only by a Divine act, or, in other words, the Pope must be rendered infallible by the special intervention of the Deity. But as the Pope receives no other ordination than that appointed for every other Bishop—an ordination the less calculated to render him infallible, inasmuch as he who imparts it is not so—we cannot ascribe to him any such superhuman attribute, unless on the authority of an express declaration from Christ. But such a declaration we have not. The mere vote of the Church can make the Pope just as little infallible as it could confer upon his primacy the character of a fundamental and divinely-ordained institution. To attempt to bestow infallibility upon the Pope by making him go through some ceremonies invented and regulated by ordinary mortals would be to make infallibility not a dogma, but a mere bureaucratic institution. It is true this would be only following the example of those who look upon the Syllabus as a dogmatic decision, though, in reality, it is but a diplomatic document communicated by the Cardinal Secretary of State for Foreign Affairs through his envoys to various foreign Courts."

In addition to these literary announcements of opinion we have to record an address sent by the leading ecclesiastics of the diocese of Paderborn to their Bishop, the notorious partisan of the Pope in the Council. The address declares against infallibility, and entreats the Bishop to conform his attitude to the wishes of his chapter and flock. A similar prayer is most urgently submitted to the same dignitary by a Catholic gentleman from his diocese, who, in a long letter to the *Kreuz Zeitung*, dilates upon the damage that must be necessarily inflicted upon the orthodox interest were so absurd a proposition palmed upon the world as an article of faith. In his opinion the Pope and the bishops supporting him will incur a fearful responsibility, if by their making a doubtful and perfectly unnecessary addition to the Creed, thousands and thousands of souls should be driven into apostasy and eternal perdition.

In conclusion, I will append a few lines from the Berlin *Volks Zeitung*, giving a good idea of the sarcastic complacency displayed by the Rationalists in witnessing the split in the Council:—

"It is a good joke, indeed, to call the Opposition members at the Council Liberals because of their reluctance to bow to Papal infallibility. In reality, the contest raging at Rome is not between blind belief and rational enlightenment, but between two equally reactionary parties, both arrayed on the side of blind belief, and wrangling only which of them is to have the privilege to dictate it. It is not a struggle of reason *versus* authority, but a mere party dispute in the bosom of the Establishment to decide which of the opposing factions is to be paramount. However, it is quite an interesting spectacle to see them at loggerheads, and as they are both likely to issue from the combat with strength considerably impaired, we have every reason to be satisfied."

No doubt, the Rationalists would exult, were the Pope to be declared, and to declare himself, a god. What a strength it would give to their own theories, were one of their most implacable adversaries to commit himself to such an unprecedented extent! What hopes for accelerating the contemplated overthrow of all religion would they derive from so injudicious a step, were it really taken by the most ancient representative of Christianity in Europe! All which is perfectly understood by orthodox Catholics in this country. Within the last two months more than one urgent remonstrance has been privately sent to Rome by eminent Catholic noblemen and gentlemen, from Berlin, Breslau, and Cologne. Thus far, however, no impression seems to have been wrought upon the aspiring and enthusiastic Pontiff.

BERLIN, *January* 29, 1870.

CHAPTER XXIII.

THE FREEMASONS AND THE ŒCUMENICAL COUNCIL.

In the more progressive countries of the world the Freemasons have long ceased to head popular opposition against religious intolerance. North of the Po, the Pyrenees, and the Balkan, public opinion has become a power in this nineteenth century of ours, which on this one point, at any rate, needs no longer a special society for its guidance. It is, therefore, all the more calculated to claim our attention if, after a protracted and seemingly inviolable silence, a Lodge of this ancient fraternity finds itself called upon to deviate from the secluded habits of the Order, and publicly take up a gauntlet thrown down to all advocates of progress. The Grand Lodge at Baireuth, in the central or Protestant portion of Franconia (now subject to Bavaria, formerly Prussian), has issued the following public circular to its members:—

"As a rule, the Society of Freemasons takes no part in the political and ecclesiastical contests of the day.

Being a league established for moral purposes common to the whole human race, it unites, by the ties of common brotherhood, men of various political parties and different religious belief. But we cannot be expected to abide in our neutral position when the very existence of our society is attacked, or when those moral truths are imperilled which the human race has at last come to acknowledge, and which are indispensable to them if their destination is to be attained. In such a case the interest of self-preservation and the duty of vindicating those sacred truths compel us to be up and doing. On these grounds we cannot but direct your attention to the designs hatching at Rome in these latter days, and endangering the peace and the intellectual progress of civilized humanity. There is no doubt that these designs partly proceed from and partly are supported by the Order of the Jesuits, for many years past the mortal enemy of our fraternity.

"Were the Council, to which all his Bishops have been convened by Pius IX., to confine its action to the discipline of the Church, or the duties of the Catholic clergy, we should have no occasion to interfere. Even the notorious intention of the Pope, by a new dogma, to secure for himself the so-called Infallibility, concerns us less than it does the various Sovereign States of the civilized world, whose independence and liberty may be jeopardized by a human being arrogating to himself superhuman authority. As for ourselves, Infallibility, being based upon an ecclesiastical dogma, can have no convincing or binding force on the members of the society, since the moral law, which is the supreme standard of our actions, is not dependent upon any ecclesiastical authority, but solely upon truths intelligible to the human reason. All we feel called upon to do in the present emergency is to vindicate our right to exist in defiance of the Pope, who denied it in his Allocution of September 25, 1865, and in defiance of the Council, if, as is probable, the sentence of condemnation passed by the Pope should be ratified by it.

"Devoted to the promotion of humane purposes, our society is neither a member of the Roman Catholic organization nor subject to the Roman hierarchy. As long as the State, duly observing the principles of tolerance and liberalism, protects our rights, and permits us to exist in its midst, we are indifferent to the Papal thunders. Of all the reproaches hurled against us by the Pope, we plead guilty only to this one—that we practise tolerance towards those professing other creeds than ours. If the Pope looks upon this tolerance as a crime, it, in the eyes of the civilized world, is a virtue of which we need not be ashamed. All other accusations brought against us are founded upon mistaken notions of our principles, and a false view of our aims. The Pope is utterly at fault in calling us an immoral sect, since morality is the very essence of our system. Again, the Pope is at fault when he charges us with the crime of having provoked the European revolutions and wars, for we enjoin upon our members the conscientious observance of the laws of the State, and our Lodges are temples of peace. The Pope is not less at fault when ascribing to us a most determined hatred against the Christian religion, for the great majority of our members are Christians, and our league, being a society with moral objects, venerates the Founder of the Christian religion, He having revealed to the world the highest type of moral rectitude. And the Pope is at fault in calling us enemies and contemners of God, for it is the principle of the Freemasons to adore God. Noticing these grave mistakes of the Pope in what concerns us so nearly, we cannot but arrive at the conclusion that the Pope is as fallible as anybody else.

"One of the objects for which the Council has been

called together is to condemn the so-called errors of our age enumerated and denounced some time ago in the well-known 'Syllabus Errorum' by Pope Pius IX. Most of these alleged errors we regard as important truths, approved by civilized humanity, sanctioned by modern States, and to be faithfully observed by all mankind, if it is to fulfil the destiny divinely apportioned to it. The Pope condemns all philosophy and science, present and future, which objects to be fettered and directed by his hierarchical authority. (*Syllabus*, 1—14, 57.) We, on the contrary, are convinced that science, from its very nature, is, and must be, independent of ecclesiastical authority. We have not forgotten that for all great discoveries and advancement we are indebted to the spirit of free inquiry, critical observation, and logical thought; and that humanity is scarcely possessed of a single truth, but it had to be established in spite of the opposition of the ecclesiastical authorities. The Pope also rejects freedom of religion (*Syllabus*, 15—18), which we respect as one of the most sacred possessions of mankind, as a boon which, after a thousand years' struggle and suffering, has been at last generally acknowledged, and has put a stop to compulsory professions of faith and the murderous persecution of heretics. Like his predecessor, Pope Gregory XVI., Pius IX., in his 'Encyclica' of December 8, 1866, calls liberty of conscience madness, whereas we view it as the indispensable guarantee for the truth and sincerity of the relations of the human soul to God, and as the necessary basis of a morality which relies upon itself and hates nothing so much as falsehood and hypocrisy. The Pope likewise inveighs against the free exercise of the different forms of Christianity, demanding that the Roman Catholic Church be supreme and exclusive in all countries of the earth. (*Syllabus*, 77—79.) We, on the other hand, consider the right to profess any religion in public as one of the most sacred and fundamental privileges of the human race, now that it has passed its childhood. We are certainly not surprised to find the Pope, in many of his letters, and also in the 'Encyclica,' protesting against freedom of speech and liberty of the press, which he calls a pernicious pestilence; but we are still of opinion that the great task set to mankind by God, of employing and developing their fund of intellectual capacity, cannot be solved without that freedom and that liberty. If Pius IX. declines 'reconciling the Papacy to progress, liberalism, and modern civilization' (*Syllabus*, 80), this declaration to us is another proof that the Papal doctrine is unfit to enter into and to accompany the progressive development of the human race.

"Our society is, no doubt, entitled to examine questions of such grave importance to the interests of morality. In our Lodges enlightened, temperate, and benevolent men from the various classes of society meet fraternally. As they cannot but take an earnest interest in these subjects, and as our institutions secure to them a calm and dignified discussion, and encourage open confidence, our league, more than other societies, is in a position seriously, nobly, and manfully to debate what we have enlarged upon in the above. Like the Catholic hierarchy, our society is, moreover, spread over the whole earth. Admitting with true liberality educated men from all nations, States, religions, and Churches, and uniting them into a common alliance, it is pre-eminently called upon to meet an attack on the most precious possessions of humanity, made at all points at the same time, by an equally comprehensive system of defence. We therefore request your attention to the moral and intellectual contest now going on, and desire you to notice the progress of events. The Lodges and other re-unions held according to Masonic institutions and practices, as also each member individually in his particular sphere, are called upon to perform the moral duties with that zeal and exactitude which at so serious and agitated a time are demanded of the champions of the most sacred possessions of the human race. In this expectation we extend to you our right hand of fellowship, and cordially salute you, according to Masonic rites."

If public opinion be correct in estimating the prevailing disposition of some other Lodges in Germany, not all would be inclined to endorse the language of their Baireuth brethren respecting the worth of ecclesiastical authority.

BERLIN, *January* 26, 1870.

CHAPTER XXIV.

AN ANTI-PAPAL MOVEMENT.

CLOSELY following each other's example, the most important Catholic towns of Germany have by this time declared against the enactment of Infallibility. Cologne, Bonn, and Breslau have sent congratulatory addresses to Dr. Döllinger, the Munich Professor, who was the first to take up the cudgels against the Jesuits. Münster and Trèves, with other towns in their dioceses, have memorialised their respective Bishops; and Munich itself has conferred its franchise upon the fearless advocate of Catholic freedom resident within its walls. The addresses and memorials proceeding from these cities are signed, if not by a large number, at any rate by the most eminent of the inhabitants, including many who have received priestly ordination. Among the names appearing in the Cologne address, for instance, there are the leading Government officials, judges, lawyers, physicians, headmasters, and professors of the public schools,

some wealthy merchants, and, wonder of wonders,
even the editor of a Catholic paper, publishing for the
edification of Rhineland. The teachers of religion
who have subscribed this remarkable document are,
I believe, all of them priests. Similarly, the Bonn
and Breslau addresses bear the signatures of almost
every Catholic professor of any reputation in those
places, while that emanating from Münster is distinguished for being the work of the Bishop's own prelates and prebendaries. In all these significant utterances, the subscribers, more or less directly, declare
that for the Pope to push matters to extremity, and
make himself a demigod, will be running the risk of
provoking another schism, and of driving thousands
to desert the Catholic Church. There is no doubt
that this anticipation may eventually turn out to be
correct, whatever the indifference with which the
Catholic masses have hitherto regarded the Council.
In this country Catholics may be divided into three
classes. The first comprehends the people who either
believe in the dogmas of the Church, or, at any rate,
respect it sufficiently to keep objections to themselves;
the second class are those too indifferent to care for
anything the Pope may think fit to commit or omit;
while the third consists of a small educated minority

who have not broken with their Church, but are desirous to sustain it, or as much of it as can be kept above water amid the surging flood of a latitudinarian age. Though the addresses have only issued from the last-mentioned section, still it is very possible that should a rupture ensue, large numbers of the two other classes will be roused by the kindling spark, and carried away with the enthusiasm of their intellectual betters. Such a result is the more probable, as the men now protesting against the Pope's favourite doctrine all belong to the wealthy and cultivated strata of society, whereas those yet remaining indifferent spectators of the Œcumenical display may, generally speaking, be set down as the tradespeople and villagers. In the Germany of to-day a religious movement is certainly slow to commence, but once really called forth by the unbearable arrogance of a foreign priesthood, it will, by that very indifference to religion, so long retarding its outbreak, be likely to assume considerable proportions.

In addition to the above more important addresses, I must not omit mentioning that, with the exception of one, all professors of Roman Catholic theology at the University of Prague, as well as eight other Catholic professors at the same institution, have declared in favour of Dr. Döllinger and his manly theses. As much has been done by Dr. Michelis, a professor in the Catholic seminary at Braunsberg, and by some Croat notabilities at Agram, who have sent a glowing epistle to Bishop Strossmayer, the eloquent representative of their diocese at the Council. Were he so minded, this Bishop Strossmayer might essentially contribute towards effecting a religious reform in his country—nay, among more than one tribe of Sclavonic origin and Papal creed. By his long-continued vindication of the national claims of the Sclavonic races, he has achieved such a reputation among his compatriots that his very name would be sufficient to encourage them to attempt the realization of their old desires for an independent Church. Even now his speeches at Rome are commented upon in jubilant leaders in the press of Belgrade, Agram, and Prague.

How critical the German Bishops consider the juncture may be gathered from their failing to check the opposition to the Pope.* True, most of them are themselves taking part in that opposition, and, indeed, have given it the impetus it possesses; but what

* They have since deprecated the assistance of the laity in the ecclesiastical struggle they are carrying on, but in very mild language, and only at the direct request of the Vatican.

Catholic dignitary would dream of calling in the assistance of the laity to help him in fighting brother clericals could he possibly dispense with it? That the German Bishops are setting aside the ancient and systematic pride so engrained in their caste is proof sufficient that in the present emergency they regard it as less dangerous to give the people a voice in matters ecclesiastical than let the Pope have his way unimpeded. Of all the German remonstrants only Professor Michelis, at Braunsberg, and some of the Bonn professors of theology, have been mildly called to order by their Bishops. To make up for the episcopal want of zeal in punishing his adversaries, the Pope is actually obliged to fall back upon argument, and to try to refute those whom he cannot, as of yore, silence by the strong arm. As we learn from Cologne, a member of the Episcopal Chapter there, apparently more Papally inclined than his own Bishop, has been commissioned by the Vatican to answer Döllinger's heresies in a pamphlet in German. He will have need to call all his erudition to his aid, as a special journal has just been established at Cologne for the purpose of combating the presumptions of the Roman Pontiff. This interesting addition to periodical literature, entitled *Der Rhein-*

ische Merkur, and edited by Dr. Fridolin Hoffman, is to be an orthodox Catholic organ, yet opposed to those latest endeavours of the Italian and Spanish clergy which threaten to render Catholicism an anomaly in an enlightened country. I say the Italian and Spanish clergy, as they it is who form the body guard of the Pope, and who, from their numerical strength, possess an influence in the Council warranted neither by the size nor the intellectual status of their dioceses. When it is considered that the 27,000,000 of Italians are represented by 230 cardinals, bishops, abbots, and fathers-general of monastic orders, whereas the 34,000,000 French have only eighty-four, and the 19,000,000 German Catholics no more than nineteen deputies at St. Peter's, the discrepancy is so glaring as to mock all attempts to account for it in a reasonable way. But the injustice of this arrangement towards the most cultivated Catholic countries becomes perfectly ludicrous when observing that the 3,000,000 semi-civilised Sclavonians in European Turkey have been positively allowed to send as many as twelve of their reverend fathers to the Eternal City; that Australia, which is only beginning to be inhabited, has forwarded thirteen; and that the Chinese Catholic clergy, whose flocks are still dividing their allegiance between wooden idols and the portraits of the Virgin Mary, muster fifteen. Again, the Spaniards have forty members; the South Americans, thirty; the Orientals, forty-two, &c. If the Pope thinks this an equitable division of votes, he must be of opinion that the Holy Spirit, whose presence he claims for the Council, is the stronger in the members the more ignorant the nations they represent.

BERLIN, *February* 19, 1870.

CHAPTER XXV.

GERMAN BISHOPS COMMENTING UPON THE RELIGIOUS
MOVEMENT.

Four German Bishops, all of them members of the Anti-infallibility party at the Council, have broken silence on the religious movement gradually forming in their respective dioceses. To judge from the tenor of their utterances, two are beginning to fear that from opposing an unerring Pope the public may be led farther, and end by attacking some other and more ancient institutions of the Church, dear to the episcopal heart. In such an event these Bishops who, it is well known, did not at first object to the growth of popular opposition at home, apparently looking to it for the support of their own proceedings at the Council, would be injured from the very quarter whence they expected aid. Hence remonstrance. The two alarmed Prelates are the supreme pastors of the arch-dioceses of Cologne and Munich, who, in their official organs, and with their own signatures affixed, exhort the faithful to beware of being involved in religious agitation. According to him of Cologne, the danger of any such entanglement would consist in supplying the advocates of Infallibility with a pretext for " passing an ecclesiastical vote on a subject, which in the opinion of many it is neither necessary nor advantageous to settle at the present time." The Munich dignitary does not enter into particulars, but merely contents himself with saying that the excitement prevailing on the matter has been got up artificially, and had be better allayed, as it cannot but cause disquietude to many faithful believers. I am afraid both these admonitory letters will, by the German Liberals, be regarded as confirming their impression, that in declaring against infallibility the Bishops of this country are actuated less by a rational antagonism to the irrational, than by the fear that to go to this unprecedented extremity, would be to expose their entire creed and authority to inconvenient animadversion. An even more determined stand against the Anti-infallibilists among the laity is made by another German member of the minority at the Council, Bishop Ketteler of Mayence. This right reverend gentleman, who likewise publishes a paper in the city where his diocesan throne is erected, avails himself of this handy medium to inform his flock (also under his own hand and seal) that he does not at all agree with Dr. Döllinger, who had changed from what he was, and in assuming the possibility of the true doctrine being obscured by an Œcumenical Council, in fact ceased to be a Roman Catholic. Dr. Döllinger, he goes on to assert, had attacked not only the infallibility, but also the primacy of the Pope, and was worthy of the honours heaped upon him by the enemies of Church and Holy See. In Herr von Ketteler's mouth these strictures will surprise no one. Fiery and talented, he has ever been one of the most active supporters of Ultramontanism on this side the Alps, and naturally had far other motives for dissuading the Vatican from the proclamation of the disputed dogma, than those actuating the scholarly and pious professor of Munich University. But with the ever increasing approbation of his countrymen on his side, Dr. Döllinger can afford to incur the displeasure of a Romanist ecclesiastic. It is certainly a sign of the times that at a moment when the Ultramontane representatives of the Bavarian peasantry are met in force in the Munich Parliament, Dr. Döllinger should receive so many congratulatory addresses from the cultivated classes in his own country, and Germany generally. As he acquaints us in the last issue of the *Allgemeine Zeitung*, he finds it totally impossible to answer them all separately. Perhaps as remarkable as Dr. Döllinger's opposition is the conversion to his principles of another professor of theology, a member of the same Catholic university with himself. Dr. Döllinger, an erudite scholar, has, from his profound knowledge of ecclesiastical history, been moved to speak out against Papal presumption; but Dr. Sepp, who has just avowed the same opinions with his celebrated colleague, has long been famous in this part of the world as an ardent and argumentative writer on the side of the Ultramontane interest, and, till very lately, was numbered among those who regard Rome and the Church as identical. Surely, if such a man is conscientiously moved to turn round, and begins to make a distinction between the priest and the creed, the time has come when Jesuits had better pause and consider. In a book just published by him, under the title "Projects of Church Reform," there occurs a passage, which I will cite as a specimen of the tone adopted by only a few, it is true, but these the most learned and eminent representatives of Catholicism in Germany:—

"Though all Catholics are bound to maintain the

authority of the Church, they need not acknowledge the infallibility of a single individual. It is a devilish, not a heavenly inspiration, which makes a man long for the title of an unerring judge. When the Roman emperors were deified, it certainly did not contribute to the welfare of the world, and what advantage are we now-a-days to derive from this ambiguous infallibility to be conferred upon the Pope? We will never suffer the head of the Church to be made the Dalai Lama of the Occident. We will never acknowledge the Pope as a fountain of revelation and an oracle of the Church. There is but one Logos, and Christ alone, not his pontiff, can be an object of worship. Let them have recourse to the thunders of the Vatican to attain this height of their ambition—they will yet be impotent. With the alternative placed before us of recognising such a doctrine or disobeying Rome, the most faithful will be compelled by conscience to refuse allegiance. To the best and most earnest Catholics this novel presumption is something horrid, while unbelievers actually compare it to the Apocalypse. It is a notorious fact that the government of the Church is exclusively in the hands of Italians: let the head be armed with the right to give absolute decisions, and it is to be foreseen, that the various nations will form separate Churches of their own, and that in addition to an Anglican and Gallican we shall witness the rise of a Germanic establishment. We all are aware that even a hierarchy cannot dispense with popularity.... More dogmas have arisen under the present pontificate than in the last thousand years, the gentlemen at Rome being the only ones conscious of their need of such.... For Catholics *and* Non-Catholics the enactment of infallibility will be the signal for setting to work and effecting a second dissolution of the order of Jesuits."

The writer of the above is a Catholic believer, and a Catholic professor of theology in the only Catholic capital of Germany. Need I say more?

Far different in purport from the above episcopal letters is a communication addressed by Bishop Hefele of Rottenburg to the *Stuttgart Volksblatt*. Though one of the most uncompromising antagonists of the Jesuits and their latest dogmas, the Bishop complains that the papers are better informed of what is going on at the Council than the members themselves. A signer of the Anti-Infallibility address, he yet had been unable to obtain a copy until he saw it in the public journals. He thinks this early publication an unjustifiable and not very judicious proceeding, but does not go the length of blaming the interest the public naturally take in the debates. Of the manner in which business is conducted, he says it is terribly slow ; while, as regards the new rules of the assembly, all he can do is to hope that they will not too much curtail liberty of speech.

Notwithstanding that matters are thus in a fair way of becoming critical, the Prussian Government do not feel themselves called upon to imitate the French and Austrian example, and request the Pope to consider consequences. Being a Protestant Government they believe they had better keep aloof while the question is confined to this primary stage of theological debate. Whatever the issue, they are tolerably safe from the thunders of the Pope. Should the votes of the Council lead to a collision between Church and State this Government, strong in the inbred Protestantism of the majority of its subjects, may likewise depend on the valuable assistance of the North German Catholics. I have already alluded to the attitude of the Breslau and Münster Catholic Faculties : to-day we learn that *all* the professors of Catholic theology at Bonn—the most learned body in that department in Germany—have signified their adhesion to Dr. Döllinger's views.

BERLIN, *February* 23, 1870.

CHAPTER XXVI.

RATIONALISM, CATHOLICISM, AND THE POPE.

THE moment France insisted upon the privilege properly belonging to all Catholic States of sending an Ambassador to the Œcumenical Council, the Pope lost no time in introducing the Infallibility Bill. Orders were also given to expedite the enactment of the Canons. Before, then, the Duc de Broglie, who is likely to be appointed to represent his country at the Holy City, can arrive there, the questions at issue, if not absolutely settled, will have advanced to a stage at which it will be difficult to stop them. So the crisis is drawing near, and the nineteenth century, with all its vast knowledge and enlightenment, is to witness an enterprise which, according to a German orthodox Catholic writer, is more worthy of the Dalai Lama than of the head of Christendom.* Should public opinion by this enormity be shocked out of its

* Professor Sepp, of Munich, in his new book against Infallibility, as quoted in letter of February 23.

habitual indifference to matters ecclesiastical, the political movement of the time may be destined to be partially replaced by an agitation which, in this country at any rate, will have a tendency to appeal to the very depths of man's inner nature. As to the German Governments, their action will be entirely guided by what the Pope will be pleased to do after the dangerous votes he has ordered have been passed by the Council. Should he really attempt to enforce the famous Canons which are to perpetuate the Syllabus,—should he insist upon subverting essential institutions of modern society, such as liberty of the press, liberty of instruction, liberty of conscience, &c., all Governments in this part of the world will be obliged to declare against him. Whatever their reluctance to promote Rationalism by officially declaring against the head of a recognized and time-honoured form of faith, if the Pope turns *révolutionnaire* and attacks the fundamental laws of the State, the Governments will in self-defence be compelled to resist him, no matter what the consequence to the cause of religion. But if the Pope prudently allows the canonized Syllabus to remain a dead letter, at least for the present, and keeping clear of secular affairs, contents himself with asserting Infallibility as a mere theological crotchet, the German Governments, I think, will not be over hasty to encourage such religious agitation as may be called forth by his spiritual presumption. Mere dogmatical arrogance on the part of the Holy See hurts no one; but a religious movement superadded to the political complications of the age, might be productive of a perplexing imbroglio and injure many conservative interests. In this rationalistic era a German religious movement might, indeed, become a serious affair, and in its primary results lead to anything but the advancement of truth. In Germany scepticism is so omnipotent now-a-days that were the religious malady of the age to assume an acute character, and the mind of the nation earnestly to busy itself with the subject, downright atheism would probably gain the upper hand at first, and some time have to elapse before any beneficial result could be attained. The present state of religious apathy is bad enough; but in the critical transition period from apathy to reformed belief, there might be an episode, when Infallibility, now a lethargic monster, awakening from its inert repose, might assume the offensive, and attack more than one institution of the State. Such a contingency no Government is likely to wish to bring on.

In the van of those orthodox and faithful children of the Church who in the eleventh hour are once more raising their warning voice, we find again Dr. Döllinger, the stout-hearted Munich prelate and professor. With his usual erudition he proves in a long article, inserted in yesterday's *Allgemeine Zeitung*, that the amended rules of procedure just palmed upon the Council grossly violate all precedent as established by so many previous assemblies of the kind. From the first modest and pious Synod at Jerusalem down to the Council of Trent, whenever the Bishops met, each one was permitted freely to communicate his views to the rest. For men assembled to elucidate the sublimest truths this privilege was considered all the more indispensable, as they have always been regarded as the exponents, not merely of their own individual notions, but of the views entertained by their respective flocks. More than this, no dogma has been ever laid down by any Council if more than a couple of dissentient voices declared against it. In nearly every instance perfect agreement was secured before decisions of the like importance were put to the vote, the *consensus omnium* being held to be the very thing testifying to the presence of the Holy Ghost in their midst. Now, compare to this the amended rules of Procedure issued by Pio Nono. In accordance with them a member can be silenced at any moment by the presiding Cardinal, and a dogma voted by simple majority. Supposing three hundred and fifty-one members were to declare in favour of Infallibility, against three hundred and fifty dissentients, Infallibility, according to Pio Nono, would legally become a doctrine of the Church, notwithstanding its rejection by nearly half the reverend representatives. It is true, the Council rejoices in the presence of too many Oriental and Italian Bishops to run the risk of exposing the unprecedented nature of these Papal proceedings in all their hideousness; yet as there are about two hundred dissentients in an assembly of seven hundred, and as those two hundred happen to belong to the most civilized nations, in striking contrast to the pious enthusiasts and ignorant bigots opposed to them, the working of the new by-laws will produce quite as anomalous results as though the votes were more equally divided.

As a first symptom of popular sympathy with the Pope, the Central Committee of the Catholic Societies in the Diocese of Mayence has issued an address against Dr. Döllinger and his adherents. This being —to my knowledge—about the only document of the kind extant, whereas thousands of the most respectable signatures figure in the opposition addresses, it will not go far in improving the Papal prospects. The high-sounding name of "Catholic Societies" is supposed to cloak a semi-ecclesiastical brotherhood, chiefly recruited from the humbler classes. These Societies have been frequently, but always in vain, asked to publish a list of their members. The other day the demand was repeated by some orthodox, anti-Syllabus professors at Breslau, yet again failed to elicit a reply.

The Russian Press is in a perfect state of exultation at the blunders committed by the Pope. Catholicism, whose most important feature to them is its identification with Polonism in their part of the world, will, they hope, be materially damaged by the Council.

BERLIN, *March* 12, 1870.

CHAPTER XXVII.

PRUSSIA AND THE POPE.

PUBLIC opinion begins to be somewhat engrossed by the venturesome proceedings of the Pope. The Press as well as society are rife with the prolific theme of Infallibility. The Conservative papers regret that his Holiness, from perverted enthusiasm if not excessive ambition, should have been led to compromise the most ancient of the established creeds. The Radical Press, on the contrary, rejoices at his not listening to the warnings of cautious and worldly-wise counsellors, but, like a consistent simpleton, fully working out his irrational principles; while moderate organs, loathing the language of their more advanced contemporaries, yet unwilling to oppose them, preserve a significant silence. Very remarkable, too, is the attitude of the journals of the Prussian Government, which are unanimous in representing the Papal procedures as foolish, and in promising the German Bishops their best assistance should a crisis supervene. Could the Prussian

Government be but sure that the German Bishops will hold out, and really vote against the statutes they have opposed in their preliminary stages, it is probable that more than mere promises would be tendered them in the present juncture. For in such a case it might become morally certain that the Pope, though he had his canons duly enacted, would yet, by the united resistance of the German Bishops and Governments, be made to shrink from carrying them out, at least in these civilized latitudes. But the worst is, there is no telling how many of the Bishops will remain true to themselves, now that things are coming to a head. The estimate taken of their character in this correspondence seems but too correct. No sooner does the Pope show that he is determined to have his way than a large number of his episcopal antagonists are betraying an inclination to veer round and vote with the Council and its Head, rather than bring on a rupture in the Church. Such is the tenour of our latest intelligence from Rome : such, it is thought, the proof incontrovertible that, in declaring against Infallibility at all, many Bishops were not inspired by devotion to unchanging principle, but only by a prudent wish not to shock the liberal convictions of the age. Now that they are impotent to prevent the latter alternative, they are supposed to prefer siding with the Church, in which their interests centre, to vindicating, at the risk of a schism, what the world gave them credit for considering the truth. It is apprehended that when Infallibility is put to the vote scarcely a third of the two hundred opposing Bishops will be found to negative it. Owing to this melancholy anticipation, the French Government will probably not insist upon the right decidedly belonging to them of sending a representative to the Council. What, indeed, would be the use of warning the Infallible one, and encouraging his timid opponents? The former stands committed to his open avowals, and the latter are demonstrating that, however odious the Papal vagaries, they are less distasteful to them than an alliance with Liberalism, which continued resistance would entail.

In one of the articles in which the semi-official *Nord Deutsche* has lately criticized the Pope a remark occurs which deserves to be cited. The argument on which the Pope, in the Bill laid before his Ecclesiastical House, bases his claim to Infallibility, is Christ's addressing Peter as the Rock on which the Church is to be built. To this Count Bismark's organ pertinently replies, by a reference to the many and grave instances in which the favoured Apostle, as recorded in the

Gospels, proved his Fallibility, even after the distinction conferred upon him. The article winds up by hoping that in the event of its latest pretensions hurrying on the overthrow of the Papacy, the various Christian denominations so long divided by the ascendency of Rome will again draw closer to each other.

No result has to be reported of the attempt of some Catholic societies to organize a popular movement in favour of the unerring Pontiff. One Wurtemberg and nine North German Counts are all that have raised their voices for Pio Nono since my last. It is only fair to add that the anti-Papal addresses likewise ceased the moment it became clear that the Pontiff would not be turned from his purpose. As they were mostly signed by good Catholics, anxious for their Church's weal, it was but natural that a pause should supervene after what has transpired the last week. Some of this class are intimidated by the unflinching resolve of the Vatican; others may be supposed to be on the verge of heresy without as yet having made up their minds. Hence silence.

BERLIN, *March* 15, 1870.

CHAPTER XXVIII.

PROBABLE RESULTS OF THE COUNCIL.

A FEW weeks ago Count Beust begged to dissuade the Papal Government from having the famous Canons, which are to perpetuate the Syllabus, enacted by the Council. Of the Note in which these admonitions were contained I am in a position to subjoin an abstract. Alluding to the reserve Austria and the other Catholic Powers have thus far displayed towards the Council, the Vienna Chancellor proceeds to remark :—

"The Catholic Powers, and more especially Austria and France, being anxious to leave the Church at liberty to conduct its own concerns, had not interfered with the arrangements for the Council, and resigned the right properly belonging to them of sending representatives to that assembly. In thus abstaining from all interference they had been actuated by a wish to show their respect to the Church, and likewise by a recognition of that principle of modern civilization which accorded full and unrestrained liberty to Church and State within their respective spheres. For France it had been more easy to adopt such a course than for Austria, the former, by her treaties with the Pope, being entitled to stop the promulgation on her territory of any objectionable ecclesiastical decrees, a right which the latter, by her own Concordat, did not possess. In view, therefore, of what was preparing at the Council, and remembering the protests a short time ago couched by the Austrian Bishops against the new school and marriage laws, and the agitation to which their resistance had given rise, Austria could not but feel uneasy concerning the future. It was not, indeed, the intention of the Council to enact Papal Infallibility that disquieted her, for she trusted that this doctrine, if proclaimed at all, would be expressed in a mild and merely theoretical form, similar to the one adopted by the Florentine Council, and, therefore, without much practical influence on the course of events. Nor had the State a right to object to the proclamation of other purely religious Dogmas, such as the immaculate conception and glorification of the Virgin Mary. But it was different when the Church was about to claim a permanent and comprehensive supremacy over the State, and to arrogate to herself the right of deciding which of the laws laid down by the secular powers were binding on the subject, and which not. Unfortunately, this was the stand-point assumed in the twenty-one Canons submitted to the Council, and warmly advocated by certain parties. But, not content with establishing so unacceptable a principle, the Canons proceeded at once to make use of the prerogative claimed. The Canons declared many of the fundamental laws of all modern and civilized States unsound, invalid, and, in short, accursed. The Canons anathematized liberty of religion, liberty of the press, liberty of instruction, civil marriage, and the amenability of the clergy to the criminal code, and asserted a variety of other statutes to be contrary to the laws of God and Holy Church. Now, supposing these *Schemata* to be really passed by the Council, the danger to France would be very small, as the principles denounced had been the law of the land for nearly a century, and were likely to be upheld by the common consent of society. But in Austria legislation had only recently begun to recognize the necessity of enacting these laws long introduced in France, and the consequences resulting from clerical opposition to the new statutes would, therefore, be much more unpleasant.

For this reason the Austrian Government had applied to Rome, and pointed out the disastrous results likely to arise from a struggle between Church and State. Whatever might be enjoined by the Church, the Austrian Courts of Law would not be induced to look leniently on those that broke the laws or incited others to break them. Add to this that the majority of the Austrian Bishops were opposed to the Canons, and in the event of their being passed would be subjected to the cruel alternative of either not publishing them or of doing so against their better judgment, and it could not be denied that there were many reasons for apprehending an undesirable issue. Rome should beware of throwing down the gauntlet to the civilized world."

Together with the growing courage manifested by the ecclesiastical powers, this Austrian complaint has caused the French Minister of Foreign Affairs to follow up his oft-mentioned private letter to the Vatican* by an official despatch, uttering the same warnings in an even more urgent tone. But it is all too late. If the Pope ever hesitated, he has completely got over his scruples. His enacting the New Rules of procedure proves a determination not only to crush the minority by the majority of the assembled Bishops, which was

* Count Daru's letter and despatch are given in the Appendix.

always in his power, but even to silence the remonstrants whenever he pleases. A bold, and, in his way, sincerely religious man, Pio Nono evidently despises considerations of mere worldly prudence, and feels himself called upon to challenge all that there exists of culture in this old and tolerably ripe planet of ours. Nor is he so far wrong in making light of the opposition offered by the episcopal minority in the Council. Comparatively liberal as they appear by the side of the rest, there are few among the recusant Bishops whose opposition is not mainly actuated by a dread that, were the Canons and Infallibility passed, this would tend to injure rather than benefit the Church. If they can ward off this peril, well and good; if not, it is not they who will aggravate it by standing up for religious freedom, and thus bring on another schism. Were any proof needed of this, it would be supplied by the fact that Cardinal Rauscher, the father of the notorious Austrian Concordat, and the head of Ultramontanism in Germany, belongs to the most unflinching members of the minority at Rome. Then, again, as regards Catholic Governments, the French dynasty is scarcely in a position to make an enemy of the Pope, considering that only a fourth part of the French Bishops are stanch Gallicans, while the rest, as well as the inferior clergy, are devoted to the Pope rather than the independence of their National Church. The Austrian Cabinet, on the other hand, will have to be extremely cautious and spare the feelings of the Pope and all the world beside, should a religious controversy arise. To them religious agitation, superadded to the national disputes dividing their Empire, would be no joke. Of course the Pope will not for a time insist so very rigorously upon each and every one of the Canons being carried out, or all the Governments of the world would be forced into fierce antagonism, no matter how ardent their wish to adopt a more conciliatory policy; but this sort of wisdom has never been foreign to the Vatican, which always understood to a nicety how much of its theoretical claims it dared press at a given moment. On this supposition the only real danger the Pope can have to encounter on his way will arise from public opinion revolting against the claims of a superstitious priesthood. But such an event the Holy See has long ceased to fear. Luther, relying upon the enthusiasm of a stern and devout age, may have succeeded in intimidating the purpled dignitaries of Rome; but the present period, with its slight interest in matters transcendental, does not seem sufficiently to command the Pope's respect to make him ordinarily cautious.

From his daring conduct we are free to infer that he hopes to enslave the minds of the uneducated more fully than ever, and yet not rouse the better informed from that apathy which, while it pretends to ignore him, permits him to try his worst. Will he be out in his reckoning after all? We have to-day to record some more addresses from Kreuznach, Neuss, and other Rhenish towns, declaring against Infallibility; but more is wanted than a mere protest against what is obsolete to set a religious movement a-going, and inspire that faith and earnestness without which there can be no reform.

BERLIN, *March* 20, 1870.

CHAPTER XXIX.

COMING TO TERMS.

CARDINAL ANTONELLI'S reply to the last anxious despatch of Count Beust fully confirms my anticipations as to the discreet use the Holy See intends to make of the new prerogative to be voted by the Council. "There is,"—Cardinal Antonelli has signified to the Envoy of the Austro-Hungarian Monarchy —"a great difference between theory and practice. No one will ever prevent the Church from proclaiming the great principles upon which its Divine fabric is based; but as regards the application of these sacred laws, the Church, imitating the example of its heavenly Founder, is inclined to take into consideration the natural weaknesses of mankind, and accordingly exacts only so much from human frailty as is within the power of every age and country to render." This language is in striking contrast with the comprehensive and unconditional cursing of the Canons. It replaces fanaticism by prudence, accommodates principle to circumstances, and avowedly modifies the rigidity of a supernatural code by a reasonable regard for sublunary time and locality. By this important announcement, the Pope engages himself to break the new ecclesiastical laws, wherever and whenever such infraction should appear to be conducive to the welfare of the Church. Accordingly it may be presumed that mixed marriages will be forbidden in the Tyrol, where public opinion is sufficiently bigoted to enforce the prohibition, but winked at in Hungary, whose Magyar population is too much impressed with the necessity of facing the world as a national whole to suffer artificial barriers to be erected in their midst by a foreign priest. Again, it is likely that the King of Bavaria will not be excommunicated for permitting his Lutheran subjects to profess their religion in a kingdom alleged to be specially patronized by the Holy Virgin, whereas the Government of Paraguay are sure to be told that its only alternative lies between preventing the erection of Protestant churches or going to Hell. Likewise the subjection of ecclesiastics to secular Courts will be interdicted in Bolivia, but connived at in France; while Infallibility, scarcely fit to become more than a shadowy phantom in this civilized quarter of the globe, will be carried out in downright earnest only among the more highly-coloured and less-elaborately cultivated inhabitants of the far East and West. It must be admitted that this cautious method of reconciling the novel claims of the Pope to the existing realities of the political world will tend to obviate the disturbing influence the Council might otherwise exercise upon the future of civilized States; but will Pio Nono, will his successors, be always so cautious in wielding the omnipotent sceptre as Cardinal Antonelli promises? Will not a clergy, who cannot reasonably expect to bias the educated classes, be strongly tempted to strive for power through the lower strata of society, when the million have once been taught in Church and school to revere the Pope as their God upon earth? Unless they hoped their opportunity was coming, what motive could they have for making preparations to use it? Though Pio Nono may be an enthusiast, can we believe his Jesuit eulogists to be actuated by exclusively religious motives in maintaining his supremacy over worldly affairs?

We have to record a fresh list of demonstrations against the Pope and Council. The theological Faculties of Munich, Bonn, Breslau, and Münster have already lifted up their voice and pronounced almost unanimously against the doings at Rome; the Episcopal

Seminary at Braunsberg has produced one of the most determined antagonists to Infallibility; and at this moment Würzburg University is joining the goodly array, one of its priestly Professors, a Dr. Schengg, openly declaring in his lectures that Infallibility can neither be based upon nor logically deduced from Christ's promise to Peter, as related Matt. xvi., 16-18. Würzburg has long been in the hands of the Ultramontanes, and its being infected by broader views is a fact of no small moment. At present Freiburg is the only place of importance where all the Professors are still in unison with the Pope. Professor Döllinger, at Munich, the first to set the anti-Jesuit agitation agoing, has been distinguished by fresh marks of approbation. From the circle of Schleiden, in the very orthodox district of Aix-la-Chapelle, he has received an address, bearing the signatures of many of the most respectable inhabitants, and praising him highly for his courageous conduct. Even more gratifying must have been an ovation offered by the students attending his lectures. A few days ago, when the lecture was over, one of them rose, and, premising that he had been chosen spokesman by his "commilitons," begged to assure the learned doctor of their confidence in his teaching and character, however virulent the attacks launched against him by the Jesuitic school of theologians. In answering the young man, who is one day to be a priest, and who spoke in the name of other candidates for Holy Orders, Dr. Döllinger said that all he aimed at as a professor was to enable his pupils to search and judge for themselves. He taught them what he thought to be right and true; upon them devolved the duty of testing the accuracy of his statements. As you can easily imagine his popularity has not been diminished by this modest and straightforward reply. One of the Bavarian bishops, the Right Reverend M. Senestrey, of Ratisbon, has been so irritated by Dr. Döllinger's growing ascendency over the students, as to go the length of declaring that no one who continues to attend Munich University need apply to him for Holy Orders. Does not this look as if the plague spot of schism had already broken out? Just compare the Ratisbon decree with the tone of a correspondence another Bishop— that of Rottenburg—has addressed from Rome to the Stuttgart *Volksblatt*, and you will admit that the diversity of opinion among German prelates has reached a considerable height. The Rottenburg Bishop writes as follows:—

"A petition to the Pope is being circulated among the Bishops asking him to insert in the Ave Maria the words, 'conceived without sin.' This is another instance of the extraordinary demands and importunities assailing us here. This very day the Bishop of Pekin told me at table that an individual circulating petitions of this sort had called upon him, and, strange to say, had shown him his own signature affixed to the paper. The man had cut it out from some other paper and pasted it on to the list. Perhaps it was for the same purpose that while I attended a meeting at Cardinal Rauscher's, some Italian layman, in the presence of my young servant, tore off the *carte de visite* nailed on the door of my room."

These contemptuous remarks have been loudly re-echoed by the Liberal as well as the Conservative organs of the German Protestant press. The Liberals oppose the Council from principle; the Conservatives, however much inclined to look leniently upon its failing, yet cannot help denouncing its questionable stratagems.

You will remember Dr. Friedrichs, the Secretary of Cardinal Hohenlohe at Rome, whom the Papal police ordered to leave the town, suspecting him of supplying German papers with inconvenient intelligence about the Council. As the police would not recall the order, notwithstanding the intervention of some influential personages, the Bavarian Government have appointed the objectionable Doctor *attaché* to their Embassy, thereby liberating him from the tender mercies of the Santa Hermandad. The Munich Cabinet are not at all favourable to that faction at Rome whose eccentricities threaten to throw the apple of discord among their subjects at a period made critical enough by political broils without any ecclesiastical admixture.

BERLIN, *March* 26, 1870.

CHAPTER XXX.

THE BAVARIAN ULTRAMONTANES.—I.

(*Vide* Chapter XVIII.)

THE small majority of six the Bavarian Ultramontanes secured in the last elections to the Lower House of the Munich Parliament has not been long in producing the anticipated results. So impatient were these excited champions of the Holy See to advertise their sentiments that they thought it incumbent upon them to do so even in their answer to the speech from the throne. As their King told them plainly that, although he had no wish to see Bavaria merged in the North-German Confederacy, he was yet determined to adhere to the offensive and defensive alliance already entered upon, so they must needs answer him in the same ready and undisguised manner. Provoked by this candid announcement from the throne, the Bavarian Ultramontanes introduced addresses into both Houses of their local representative assembly, insisting that the treaties establishing military alliance with Prussia, or, what is the same, with the Northern Confederacy, should be so interpreted as to render them virtually null and void. The Upper House quickly passed its address, but on asking for an audience to deliver it, was curtly told that the King would not receive a document recommending disloyal measures, and endeavouring artificially to keep up the excitement prevalent in the country. Undaunted by this ungracious reply, the Ultramontanes in the Lower House are at this moment engaged in discussing their own Address, which, if at all differing from that of the other legislative body, does so only by an even more unblushing and indiscreet recommendation to break the treaty on which Bavaria's connection with Germany rests. As a first step towards attaining their object, the Ultramontanes in the second chamber loudly demand that Bavaria, nominally leaving her relations to Prussia as they are, should yet claim the right to decide for herself, on the outbreak of a war, whether Prussia's behaviour in bringing it about has been sufficiently moral to compel Bavaria's assistance. What this means in the mouth of these men would be clear enough of itself, even did they not insist upon a considerable reduction of the Bavarian troops, and continue, directly or indirectly, to call upon France and

Austria to come and destroy the late re-arrangement of Germany. There can be no doubt as to the nature of the motives in this interesting juncture directing the action of the Bavarian Ultramontanes and the few Absolutists that are making common cause with them. Both are convinced that the loose ties at present binding the kingdom to the rest of Germany, if permitted to continue, will soon be tightened, and ultimately result in Bavaria's complete embodiment with the Confederacy. Such a consummation both look upon as the direst misfortune that could befall them. By merging the Bavarians in a common Germanic Parliament it would deprive Rome of the last spot in Germany where she is powerful enough to exercise marked political influence; by creating a common political Parliament of all Fatherland, it would inaugurate a more liberal era, and finally remove the last lingering remnants of the old, well-intentioned, and although certainly not altogether fruitless, yet obsolete system of Government.

Horrified at this prospect, and irritated by the hopes of all liberal and enlightened elements in their own State as well as in the rest of Germany, the Ultramontanes and their Ultra-Conservative allies, in their endeavours to obviate such a shocking issue, proceed to the strongest means at their disposal. The insignificant majority they possess, and the consciousness of their being mainly indebted even for this to the ignorant villagers voting in the elections against the more cultivated towns-people, instead of restraining them from vehement measures, only serves to make them the more rabid and obstreperous. As nearly all Bavarian cities, Munich included, are against them, and the next elections are as likely as not to leave them in a minority, they imagine it to be their only policy to show their colours and do their worst, while they can do anything at all. With a frankness highly commendable, were it not directed against the happiness of their struggling race, and did it not prize Rome higher than Germany, they avow their intention to separate Bavaria from her sister States, and make it the domain of a foreign ecclesiastic, absorbed in unprecedented adoration of self. It is as though the frantic intoxication which seems to have seized the whole Ultramontane world A.D. 1870 had extended even to the ordinarily quiet and undemonstrative latitude of Munich. Fortunately they are impotent to realize their foolish desires. The King of Bavaria is too cautious and too patriotic to engage in so venturesome and ignoble a course, and the Bavarian army bears the experience of the late campaign too well in mind to wish to fight on any other side except the Prussian. Add to this, that the great majority of the educated classes in Bavaria are ranged on the same side as their King and troops, and the attitude of the Ultramontanes shrivels up to the nothingness of a mere wordy row. In all probability the King will refuse to accept the address of the Lower House, as he has done that of the Upper. Should the Bavarian Commons, notwithstanding, try to reduce their army below the figure required to give effect to the treaties with this Government, Prussia has the means at her disposal to extinguish the opposition of these feeble adversaries. In a former controversy of the same kind Prussia declared the continuance of Bavaria in the Customs Union dependent upon her abiding by and properly carrying out the military treaties. The announcement sufficed to overcome all opposition. Bavarian industry, having been adapted to the tariff and wants of the Zollverein for forty long years, would be destroyed by exclusion; nor could the Bavarian Exchequer, were it to lose its share in the Zollverein receipts, make both ends meet. As to the plan broached some time ago by the Ultramontanes, of commercially separating Bavaria from the rest of the world by a special tariff or making her enter into a Customs league with Austria, it is a rhodomontade in which nobody believes. Apart from the ruin of its manufactures consequent upon separation from the Zollverein, the kingdom is evidently too small, and the extent of its frontiers too great, to be able to exclude smugglers, unless at an unproductive sacrifice of money and means; while as to joining Austria, that would be but to gain a market having a comparatively small consumption, and already supplied by manufacturers possessed of much greater capital than those of Bavaria. There would also be some inconvenience connected with participation in the Austrian paper currency troubles.

The merest allusion by Prussia to these notorious facts will suffice to prevent the vociferations of the clerical party at Munich having practical consequences. This is so certain that the only sensation which the sputterings of the Bavarian Ultramontanes awaken here, notwithstanding the noise they make, is closely akin to that smiling pity with which the civilized world looks upon the simultaneous efforts of their brethren at Rome.

BERLIN, *February* 12, 1870.

CHAPTER XXXI.

THE BAVARIAN ULTRAMONTANES.—II.

EVEN should the Bavarian Cabinet resign in consequence of the elections, any new ministers would be obliged to respect the wishes of their sovereign, who looks upon the military treaty with Prussia as the only safeguard of his dynasty amid the ruin of so many ancient and time-honoured states.* So firm is the king in this prudent view of his position, that unshaken by the success of the other party, he has just congratulated the constituency of the small town of Füssen, near his Alpine castle of Hohenschwangau, upon their returning a Liberal member. Apart from these important agencies in favour of unity, the triumph of the Ultramontanes is scarcely great enough to permit their acting wholly irrespective of the Liberals. Of the eight provinces of Bavaria, the two

* Since the above has been written, Prince Hohenlohe and two other ministers have resigned, and been replaced by statesmen cherishing principles similar to their own.

that are Protestant—the Palatinate and Central Franconia—have returned only Liberals. Another, Suabia, half Protestant, has elected about as many Liberals as Ultramontanes, while in the rest the Romanist party has gained a small preponderance. Nor ought it to be overlooked that in the capital, Munich, and some of the other large towns none but Liberal candidates obtained a majority. This is a fresh proof that even in the old, and, comparatively speaking, strictly Catholic portion of the kingdom, it is only the ignorant inhabitants of the villages and smaller towns that can be prevailed upon to oblige their priests at the poll. With the army and educated classes on his side, with the North applauding his politics, it may be hoped that the young King of Bavaria will be able to prevent his good ship of State from foundering on Ultramontane breakers.

But, futile as the exertions of the Popery party in the South promise to be in the end, it is a matter of considerable interest to watch the unremitting energy with which they swim against the stream. Could there be any doubt as to the vast importance of the change which, in more respects than one, will be wrought some day by the complete reunion of Germany, it would be removed by the resistance offered to the process in its very outset by the sworn advocates of moral and intellectual slavery. The Ultramontanes have a distinct presentiment that a common Germanic Parliament is likely to be neither a reactionary nor a radical, but a liberal and a moderate body. However cunningly the franchise might be arranged, it would never yield a reactionary result: a census would give ascendancy to the middle classes, who are liberal, and universal suffrage, after the admission of the Southerners to the Confederacy, only redound to the advantage of the Radicals. The latter alternative neither the Prussian government nor the educated strata of society will submit to; there remains, then, nothing but to adopt and promote the former. But nothing would more effectively diminish Ultramontane authority than the establishment of a temperate Administration, too liberal not to take an interest in the intellectual advancement of the people, and too independent of radical crotchets to permit haughty sects to abuse religious liberty and preach the doctrine of intolerance under the protection of laws enacted for the maintenance of the opposite principles. No wonder, then, the Ultramontanes should be shocked by the shadow of a United Fatherland looming in the distance; no wonder, that being, of all its states influential only in Bavaria, they should move Heaven and earth to organize an effective resistance to the progress of the national movement in this last remaining stronghold of their German defences. Edged on by a sort of convulsive paroxysm, they have, in those Bavarian elections, shunned no lie, no calumny, if it did but serve their purpose. Perfectly indifferent to the contempt of all respectable and educated people, whom they probably think too far gone for recovery, they have positively wallowed in falsehood, and told the poor misguided field hands who form their body guard any number of nonsensical enormities on the disadvantages of joining Lutheran and army-ridden Prussia. They have tried to revive religious hatred, to inculcate anew the old and gradually vanishing rivalry between North and South, and, as all this would have scarcely furthered their ends in these enlightened times, actually frightened their subject peasantry with the story that Prussia, to evade bankruptcy, is looking out for their pighide money bags. Just to afford a specimen of their achievements in this particular department of rhetoric, I will quote an electioneering article from the *Munich Volksbote*, a famous and favourite organ of theirs, edited for the benefit of the lower classes. Cautioning its readers not to choose Liberal members, this paper thus alludes to the dreadful consequences of a " Pro-Prussian" majority in the Chambers:—

"Have you any wish to see your king degraded to the position of a Hohenzollern vassal, a miserable prefect in the pay of the Berlin authorities? Or do you want to see the independence of this ancient and glorious country of Bavaria sacrificed for the benefit of those hungry, impoverished, and half-starved Prussians? Are you at all anxious to have your own officers removed from your own army, and superseded by the pitiful fops called Prussian lieutenants? Have you any desire to witness the transportation of the Bavarian regiments to the backwoods of Pomerania, whose very name cannot be fitly mentioned in decent society, or to famished East Prussia? And would you take delight in having our cities garrisoned by the voracious wearers of the Prussian helmet, sent to regale themselves in our larders and to propagate Prussian morality at the expense of the honesty of our women? Are our constitutional liberties to be destroyed by the Prussian cat-o'-nine-tails? Is the coarse, brutal, and infamous military rabble, that forms the army of our Northern neighbour to infect our gallant troops with its spirit of haughty wickedness? Will you consent to see your pockets emptied to the last penny, and yourselves skinned into the bargain, in order that Prussia may fulfil its Divine mission? And you, inhabitants of Munich, what would you say if your picture galleries were stripped of their contents, and all the famous works of art, in whose possession you have so long gloried, carried off to Berlin? Are the magnificent monuments adorning your public squares to be pulled down and recast into Prussian guns? Is Munich really to become a provincial town, deserted by your court, unknown to strangers, the abode of abject misery and penury? Is civil marriage to be introduced into this Christian country? Are your schools to be demoralised and become nests of Paganism? Are your churches to be turned into brothels, where modern goddesses of Reason are adored by sensual devotees? No, you will not permit these abominations. You will, on the contrary, stand up for Bavaria," &c., &c.

A nice catalogue of delinquencies to be committed by the Prussians if ever paramount in Bavaria. But the event is hardly likely to happen to-morrow, and in the meantime it is a good thing that these unscrupulous marauders are degenerate enough to be roused to no more serious emotion than a laugh, by prophecies like the above. Instead of resenting the delineation given of their character, the wicked people of this country are positively amused at having reduced the Ultramontanes to a position tacitly admitted to be desperate by the very excess to which these rantings are carried. The Prussians certainly regret that the Ultramontane majority in the Bavarian Chamber will have the power to render the military alliance between the two countries less practically useful than it might be; but they are also aware that the Ultramontanes will be impotent to annihilate the important treaty, and are perfectly content for the time being to let the matter rest here. Should the Bavarian army be ever summoned to support the Prussians, it is not the illiterate peasantry of the Bavarian Alps and plains that will prevent it, nor are the clergy of their lonely hamlets likely to exercise any marked influence on the progress of the world's affairs, when the day dawns on which the general condition of Europe will admit of the complete unification of Germany.

BERLIN, *February* 20, 1870.

CHAPTER XXXII.

INCREASING OPPOSITION.

CATHOLIC society begins to shrink from the goings on at Rome. Like vigilant sentinels astir long before the main body is aroused from its drowsy slumbers, the more sensitive minds feel the provocation offered by the Pope. In many an indignant breast the displeasure awakened by his eccentric proceedings is too warm, to be allayed by his promise, that he will use his new powers with the utmost discretion and leniency. The idea of having infallibility and the thousand alleged sins of the civilised state daily set forth in Church and school, even thought his stupendous doctrine may not be employed to foment actual rebellion, is yet clearly too much for many a latitudinarian, nay, for many a devout Catholic. Men, apparently too far gone in unbelief to care for anything the Pope might advance, or else too blindly attached to the Church to doubt even her wildest teachings, are gradually adopting a new set of opinions, and manifesting a moral repugnance to what is felt to be too bad for endurance. Certainly feelings such as these, are, as yet, to be met with only in the upper and more highly cultivated strata of the middle class, and in this are confined to a minority, small though daily increasing. Possibly, they will never extend to the lower and less susceptible grades; possibly it will take some time to make them sufficiently prevalent even among the intelligent and reflecting, for any practical result to be worked out. But should reform be attempted, it would assuredly derive considerable impetus from the warmth created in this present preliminary stage of sullen discontent. How potent this feeling has already become you may infer from the fact of the Rev. Dr. Weiser, Secretary to the Papal Mission at Munich, finding it necessary to contradict a rumour charging him with the authorship of the Bavarian letters in the *Unita Cattolica*. The *Unita*, a journal published under the patronage of the Pope, has been the *Moniteur* of the Infallibility Commission from the outset and ever since the inauguration of the present Pontifical policy waged a fierce war against all antagonists, open and unavowed. Among others, the Bavarian Government has come in for a considerable share of its righteous anger. If to maintain his position in Munich society a Papal Secretary of Legation is obliged to deny all connexion with so authoritative an organ, the Pope, one is led to conclude, cannot retain his former ascendancy over the Bavarian mind. As much may be guessed from the King of Bavaria continuing to write demonstrative letters against the Holy See. His last two missives were addressed to Father Hölzl, a Franciscan monk, whom he congratulated for defending Döllinger, and to Professor John Huber, also a Bavarian clergyman, famous for exposing the shortcomings of the Papacy in the *Allgemeine Zeitung*. A relation of this professor, Dr. Franz Huber, has achieved notoriety by sending a curious challenge to Pater Roh, one of the best known Jesuits in Germany. The Pater, it appears, repeatedly asserted in the pulpit that the doctrine ordinarily attributed to his order of the end justifying the means has never been professed by them. In reply to this, Dr. Huber offered to prove that the world was right in believing of the Jesuits what it does, desiring at the same time the rev. Pater to choose any one learned faculty as umpire between them. The Pater not deigning to take up the gauntlet, Dr. Huber thought it expedient to change the tone argumentative for one more forcible, and in a fresh letter to his adversary, accosted him in these uncomplimentary terms:—" Your declarations in the pulpit are mere Jesuitical bravado, and your present silence is a token of your want of honourable feeling. If you are a man, you will, after this, sue me for libel." This the Pater has till now omitted doing. All Bavaria animadverts on the dispute.

Similar symptoms, which if the Pope were not above watching mere terrestrial events would not escape his notice, are reported from various parts of Northern Germany. At Leipsic, Dr. Schenk, a professor of Botany in the University there, by extraction a Bavarian Catholic, has embraced Protestantism for the avowed reason that he will not subscribe to the goings on at the Council. At Cologne, the *Rhenish Mercury*, a paper expressly established to protest against the exaggerated demands of the Papacy, is adopting a more and more sarcastic tone against adversaries evidently held to be too far gone astray from the ordinary laws of reason and logic to deserve any more serious mode of treatment. In a recent issue, this journal, which professes to be orthodox withal, begs to inquire whether a Pope would remain infallible if he should happen to go mad; or whether infallibility, in such an emergency, would revert to the

Church and, if so, who was to decide on the exact moment of the transfer. Again, if the Pope asserted his sanity, despite his being considered a madman by ordinary mortals, would it be possible to contradict him, considering that an infallible mind was, perhaps, subject to other laws than fallible ones? Or was it peradventure to be regarded as the only conclusive proof of a Pope's insanity if he declared against the Jesuits? As the Jesuits accounted for Clement XIV. abolishing their society by proclaiming him a lunatic, would every other Pope inimical to their interests be likewise regarded as a madman, and be stripped of his divinity accordingly? These and similar questions are asked in more than one paper. What has become of the ancient reverential respect for the Pope, if such quibbles can be raised at his expense in temperate Catholic organs?

To refute the infallibilists with evidence supplied by the Church itself, a Silesian priest has addressed an interesting letter to the editor of the *Breslauer Zeitung*. In lieu of all learned discussion, he simply contents himself with quoting an article published no less than fifty-one years ago in the *Tübingen Theological Review*, a learned and most respectable Catholic organ, which would indeed appear to supply a valuable contribution to the controversy. I will only extract the following from it :—

"Some Protestant theologians having lately twitted us upon the alleged infallibility of the Pope, we find it necessary to declare that never has the Catholic Church acknowledged any doctrine of the kind. Even the devoutest adherents of Rome never dared to advance such an axiom. If there were some few Jesuits longing to bestow this boon upon the Pope they never dared to call it a tenet proclaimed, or even so much as admitted, by the Church. All Church history proves such a thing never to have been accorded the Pope, to confirm which we refer the reader to Cotta's *Commentatio Historico-Theologica de Fallibili Pontificis Romani Auctoritate, ex Actis Concilii Constantiensis maximum partem deducta. Lugduni Batavorum*, 1732. Were any further evidence necessary we might cite the fourth clause of the *Declaratio Cleri Gallicani* in 1682, in which the decisions of the Pope are declared as admitting of amendment, even when given on matters of faith."

Disquieted by some attempts of the Jesuits to introduce themselves again into their country, the Swiss Federal Government have reminded several cantons that the Order is excluded from holding office in church and school in Switzerland. As it required a civil war to get rid of them, the Swiss are not likely to admit the fraternity again.

BERLIN, *April* 16, 1870.

CHAPTER XXXIII.

LATEST ASPECTS.

In Silesia three more priests have publicly declared against infallibility, which they denounce as contrary to the dogma and dignity of the Church. From the straightforward language in their pronunciamentoes, they appear to be acting under the impulse of strong moral disgust. One of these recusants has been suspended from office by the Episcopal Vicariate; the two others remain in the uninterrupted enjoyment of their stipends, and are permitted to minister at the altar and the font, as heretofore. If the hesitation which the Breslau ecclesiastical authorities experience in punishing dissent is observable in this very dissimilar treatment of identical cases, it is no less manifest in a circular missive they have just addressed to the whole of their diocesan clergy. Far from openly pronouncing in favour of the contemplated addition to the Catechism, they only seem to say in this pastoral letter, that infallibility must not be attacked as long as it is a mere proposition and not yet a dogma of the Church. Utterances like those of the above courageous priests are also heard from the Suabian clergy, who are called upon by the Stuttgart press to satisfy the demands of the German national conscience, and inaugurate another secession from Rome, the seat of a foreign, coarse, and insolent theology. We have plainly before us the symptoms of the clergy awakening to a sense of their difficult and discreditable position in having to carry out the dread decrees of the Council. The movement began nine months ago, when the German bishops assembled at Fulda to couch a mild protest against the designs of their aspiring colleagues in Rome; but it is only now extending to their subordinates, and in proportion as it reaches the mere rank and file of the ecclesiastical host, naturally loses the aristocratic reserve which marked the first steps of the purpled and mitred dignitaries. Yet we must not be sanguine as to its immediate results. The Popish priesthood of this country, were they to resist the Pope, would have as much to fear from the support of the Rationalists, as they would have to suffer from their attacks if siding with His Holiness. In the former alternative they are pretty sure, by these heterogeneous allies to be led away to a sphere of modern thought, far beyond that which the most liberal among them wish to introduce into their creed; in the latter, reason, science, and devotion alike will become their irreconcilable enemies. With this Scylla and Charybdis before them, which way will they turn? Both being equally perilous, it may be surmised that, a few impulsive characters excepted, the priests will probably espouse that side, which, while no worse than the other from a religious point of view, has so many secular advantages to recommend it. Before any considerable number of priests can resolve to head a crusade against the Pope, they must be convinced that there exists a numerous class of devotees who, however much opposed to the new-fangled doctrines of the Holy See, are yet sufficiently orthodox to remain Catholics though they may discard Pio Nono. But I very much doubt their believing in the existence of such a class. Living in the intellectual atmosphere of this country, they must regard it as morally certain, that in the event of a Catholic reform being attempted by anyone, whether priest or layman, it will issue in something very different to mere rejection of infallibility. If, then, reform is to ensue at all, it is ten to one that it will ensue in the secular rather than the ecclesiastical body, and that the manly manifestoes of individual priests will of themselves have no power to influence the generality of their cautious and diffident order.

But will there be any reform at all? With the experience of the last nine months before us, we can weigh the chances. First, as regards the impetus that might be given by the governments opposing the meddlesome politics of the Pope, we have Cardinal Antonelli's promise, that his master, for the present at any rate, will content himself with a mere theoretical supremacy over the Kings and nations of the earth. The governments, therefore, are not likely to move, as long as they can help it. Nor will the priests be more eager in opening the battle. Though many of them are undoubtedly ashamed of having to teach infallibility in church and school, and moreover, dread the consequences of outraging common sense and religion by so absurd and blasphemous a doctrine, the priests are tied to their exacting master by the fear of subverting the entire ecclesiastical fabric, the moment they declare against any portion of it. And the laity? The masses are mute. Thinking Catholics, on the other hand, if orthodox, are restrained by the same motives as the priests, or if rationalistically inclined, are indifferent to whatever enormities may be resolved upon at the Vatican. Such, at any rate, up to this moment remains the disposition of the majority among the educated. The minority in this class has far other views. Whether devout or otherwise, they are daily becoming more alive to the indignity of remaining members of a Church, which has waited for the nineteenth century to place a demigod at her head. From them religious progress among the German Catholics is most likely to emanate. But they can only set the stone rolling. It will require the active sympathy of a much wider section of society effectively to prolong the movement. Only in the event of moral disgust at the Papal proceedings growing strong enough to overcome either the fear of rationalism prevailing among the pious, or the antipathy to matters religious rife in latitudinarian circles—can a permanent reform take place. The day of this retributive consummation, although we may not live to see its ultimate result, is yet visibly drawing near. It might be considerably accelerated by a corresponding revival in the Protestant Church. Or perhaps it will precede, and give the signal for, such a revival. Its exact date will be determined by the course of domestic and foreign politics, by the feelings, passions and resolves of many millions, or, possibly, by the inspirations of a few leading dictatorial minds.

BERLIN, *May* 7, 1870.

APPENDIX.

A.—LETTERS TO THE EDITOR, TOUCHING THE STATE OF THE PROTESTANT CHURCH IN GERMANY.

TO THE EDITOR OF "THE TIMES."

Sir,—Your "Own Correspondent" at Berlin has censured the religious belief of the majority of Protestants in Germany, and he has not done so without giving his reasons for believing that censure to be well merited. Allow me to confute his arguments by opposing facts to facts.

For the sake of argument I will accept as a fact that "three-fourths, of all educated men in Germany are estranged from the dogmatic teaching of the Christian creed." Nor will I dispute the honesty of the writer's assertion that no one who "knows modern Germany will call it a Christian land, either in the sense Rome gives to the term or in the meaning Luther attached to it." I assume your correspondent to be an Englishman who has not been long enough in Germany to know that those who call themselves Lutherans form a minority far more insignificant than the extreme High Church or Ritualistic party in England, with which party, however, they must be absolutely identified on all essential points.

I will give you an instance. A few months ago a Lutheran clergyman of note stated, on a public and solemn occasion, and in the presence of many Protestants not belonging to the so-called Lutheran fraction, that while the Lutherans do drink the real blood of Christ when partaking of the Holy Communion, the Protestants of all other denominations drink only wine.

The great majority of Christians has not so learnt Christ, or the Bible which Luther gave to the people. What Luther's views on this point were is well known, and three-fourths of German Protestants do not share that opinion, but protest against it, as now exactly three hundred and fifty years ago the great Reformer Zwingli commenced to do so. By him was created that great Reformed party in Protestant Germany, of which your correspondent says nothing, except that he includes it among the three-fourths of what he ventures to call unbelieving Protestants. To be a Christian, according to his assertion, means either to be a Romanist or a Lutheran.

That kind of Christianity is indeed denied in the land of the Reformation by very many, though not quite three-fourths, of its inhabitants. I thank your correspondent for his very correct statement that the dogmatism of St. Athanasius and the statutes of the Council of Nice have entirely ceased to be a living power. What the dogmas of the Bible are, and to what part of the world its leading doctrines can be traced, these are indeed important questions, on which I for one do not expect enlightenment from your correspondent at Berlin.

As a son of the late Baron Bunsen, who caused it to be declared at his funeral by the officiating Lutheran clergyman that he died as a son of the Reformed or non-Lutheran Church,

I have the honour to sign my name as, Sir,

Yours sincerely,

ERNEST DE BUNSEN.

London, *August* 14, 1869.

TO THE EDITOR OF "THE TIMES."

SIR,—When I read the letter of your own correspondent in Berlin on that shocking event in the Cathedral there, and the reflections he makes upon it on the present state of religion in Germany, I was struck with the truthfulness of the latter. Being at present in this country, and having frequent opportunities of giving statements on the same subject, and of answering questions with regard to it, I appear sometimes as exaggerating and taking a too gloomy view of this matter. How much satisfaction did I find, therefore, that my views and those of my numerous brethren of our denomination are so fully corroborated by one whose observations are so extended and clear!

I regret, at the same time, to find Mr. de Bunsen at variance with these views, as I entertain a high regard for him personally, as well as on account of his late very excellent father. But I cannot refrain, for truth's sake, from contradicting his statement "that those who call themselves Lutherans form a minority far more insignificant than the extreme High Church or Ritualistic party in England." If he means the so-called "Old Lutherans," he is right; but it is a fact that just at present a very serious struggle is

U

going on between the Lutheran party generally against the Union Church, now the State Church of Prussia, and some minor States of Germany. This Union consists of Lutheran and Reformers' Churches, which have "the *consensus* of their respective Creeds" as their standard. Now, the Lutheran party strive with all their might towards the dissolution of this union, being strengthened by entirely Lutheran countries, such as Saxony, Hanover, and Schleswig-Holstein, who hold fast to the exclusive views of Luther; and it may even be doubtful whether they will not succeed in dissolving the said Union, or, at least, limit it considerably.

However, I fully agree with your correspondent that all these movements are confined to a very limited fraction of our nation as a whole, and that they are slighted and even contemned by the great majority. Still, I do not undervalue in the same degree those religious communities which your correspondent calls "a sprinkling of faithful believers in every part of the country," pointing in particular to the Wupperthal, which he calls "a tower of Lutheranism," but which more properly might be called a tower of Reformed belief. I feel assured also that Berlin itself presents such a tower of excellent men in the ministry (though these are more Lutheran in their views), surrounded by many faithful believers; and so Würtemberg and other parts of the country may be pointed to in a similar sense; nor will your readers doubt that I also consider our Baptist denomination, with its seventeen thousand professing members spread over our country, as a power of great influence on our nation, while, at the same time, your correspondent is right in estimating all these combined efforts as very small in comparison with the great majority of our people, so that it is an undoubted fact that "only a small fraction of the nation attend Divine service."

I have the honour, Sir, to subscribe myself,
Yours respectfully,
G. W. LEHMANN,
Pastor of the Baptist Church in Berlin.

WALTHAMSTOW, *August* 17, 1869.

TO THE EDITOR OF "THE TIMES."

SIR,—As your journal is not the place to discuss theological opinions, I forbear to make any remarks on those expressed by your Berlin Correspondent in your issue of August 14; but, as one who has resided for some time in Germany and has interested himself in the religious condition of that great country, permit me to say a few words as to the facts to which your correspondent alludes.

It is too true that there is a sad lack of any dogmatic faith among a large portion of the German community, but it is no less true that matters in this respect are much better than they used to be formerly. Infidelity in the last century spread from the Universities to the clergy, and thence among the people, but now the Universities are much more orthodox in their tone; I might almost say the majority of the professors are believers in our common Christianity, and the clergy are most decidedly more orthodox in the main. The leaven, however, of an extreme Ritualism has been widely spread among the people, and it is not to be wondered at if they are in general passive disbelievers in the doctrine of the Trinity and the other distinctive articles of the Christian faith.

But even among them there is a reaction, and much good is doing in a quiet way. Your correspondent might have alluded to the mission carried on for the last few years with much success among the cabmen of Berlin, and the marvellous growth of Sunday Schools in Berlin and other towns of Germany, all of which date from the last five or six years.

The political condition of Prussia has had much to do with the present state of the masses. A few years back the leading evangelical preachers were all connected in politics with the extreme Tory party, which upheld the divine right of Kings. Hence the mass of the Liberal party were opposed to orthodoxy on account of its political aspects, and even the sermons of the great Krummacher were neglected. The times are changing. There is a Liberal-Evangelical party as well as a Tory-Evangelical, and inasmuch as the relation in which the Church stands to the State has been a hindrance in several places in the great Fatherland to free aggressive evangelical action, a feeling in favour of the separation of the Church and State has sprung up even in evangelical quarters. In proof of this, I might refer to the articles in the *Neue Evangelische Kirchenzeitung* on the Irish Church question. There is also a growing feeling among the Liberal party in favour of disestablishment, and I believe that so far from such a course endangering the real interests of the Church in Germany, it would lead to an outburst of Evangelical zeal, which would surprise many who look upon Germany as a land of infidels, which it decidedly is not.

As to the want of aspirants for the ministry, I cannot

think that can be the case, seeing that the religious, and in many places a good part of the secular, teaching in German schools is in the hands of the *candidaten*, who have to wait often till beyond thirty years of age before they obtain a ministerial position.*

On the whole, Sir, I look forward to a speedy triumph of the ancient dogmatic Christianity in Germany. It is a pity that the Confession of Lutheranism was not embraced in a shorter compass than the Augsburg Confession and the accompanying documents, as the length of those documents is a difficulty in requiring a strict adhesion to their letter or spirit.

Yours very truly,
CHARLES H. H. WRIGHT, M.A.,
Chaplain of Trinity Church, Boulogne,
Late British Chaplain at Dresden.

August 16, 1869.

TO THE EDITOR OF "THE TIMES."

Sir,—Allow me to correct a misprint which occurs in my letter which you kindly inserted in your journal of to-day, in which I am made to say that "the leaven of an extreme Ritualism has been widely spread among the people," instead of "the leaven of an extreme Rationalism."

In reply to the further remarks of your Berlin correspondent, permit me to say that he judges the Berlin clergy and the orthodox German theologians very erroneously when

---

* That there is a want of aspirants for the ministry, is confirmed by General Roon, the Prussian Minister of War, in a decree dated January 6, 1870, referring to this circumstance as a reason why theological students shall continue to be practically exempt from military service. [Author's note.]

he ascribes their growth in orthodox opinions to their fears of a second recurrence of the scenes of 1848. Any one who is in the habit of studying German theology can trace the steady growth of sounder views, from the time of Schliermacher onwards. The German theologians are certainly not led to adopt their theological opinions by craven fears of disastrous results from an embracing of the opposite views. However much they may have erred, or do err, they are led by the desire of discovering truth, or what they think to be so. And no one acquainted with the writings of Dr. Tholuck of Halle or Dr. Dorner of Berlin, still less who has had the pleasure of personal intercourse with them, can doubt their full sincerity and earnestness in combating Rationalistic views. They have written against Rationalism because they have felt and known that it is error, and not from any fear of the multitude.

Too much has been made of the answer which in an unguarded moment a German pastor made regarding movements of the earth. It was a reply extorted at the moment, and harped upon ever since by the Rationalist organs; but no one acquainted with German pastors can imagine that they have so little intelligence as to believe such notions of a bygone age.

The clergy are returning to orthodoxy; it will be the work of many years to lead back the people. Meanwhile, even among them there is a considerable reaction towards truth, and the number of intelligent German laymen who believe the truth is by no means small.

Yours very truly,
CHARLES H. H. WRIGHT, M.A.

Boulogne-sur-Mer, *August* 17, 1869.

TO THE EDITOR OF "THE TIMES."

Sir,—My letter to you having called forth several interesting replies, allow me to state that I accept your very well-informed Berlin Correspondent's frank explanation that when he expressed his opinion that Germany was no longer a Christian country he meant that it was not Christian "in the sense attached to the term by any Protestant creed whatsoever." If the creeds, or any of them, be taken in their literal sense, this is perfectly true. The majority of German Protestants believe that at no time any persons were or could have been authorized or capable to lay down rules for the interpretation of Scripture, which rules were to be for ever binding on the conscience of mankind. It is well known that two essentially different methods of interpretation co-existed in the early Christian Church. The more free interpretation was represented by Clement of Alexandria, Origen, and St. Jerome; the narrower one by St. Augustine. Among the representatives of these schools in Germany were Zwingli and Luther; in England, the Dutch Erasmus and Collet. The more enlightened an age is, the more will uniformity be a bar to religious unity.

I am, Sir, yours sincerely,
ERNEST DE BUNSEN.
London, *August* 21, 1869.

TO THE EDITOR OF "THE TIMES."

Sir,—I have read with much interest the letters of your Berlin correspondent which have led to discussion on this topic. The results of my own observations during a former residence in Germany and at the present time agree fully with his statements; and, while much has been written on this topic, I have read nothing which more faithfully describes the present state of affairs. The condition of religion here is, in the view of every evangelical Christian, simply deplorable. The reaction against Rationalism in some of the Universities has utterly failed to influence the masses, the sum of whose religion is, as your correspondent asserts, a vague and dim idea of the existence of a God. The Protestant clergy, instead of being looked upon with respect by the people, as in England and America, are here resented with contempt, as a sort of spiritual policemen or religious scavengers. They do no pastoral visiting, and, unless eloquent in the pulpit, have no influence in the community. They are upheld simply by the power of the State, and were this withdrawn there would be no religious reformation. On the contrary, leading ministers of Saxony have admitted to me that, if the hand of the State were withdrawn, the majority of the people would renounce even the outward forms of Christianity, as they have already renounced its truth. It is but just to say that the statements of Mr. Wright, of Boulogne, are strikingly inaccurate, and (no doubt unintentionally on his part) calculated to mislead the public.

I have the honour to be, Sir, your obedient servant,

JOHN ANKETELL,
Rector of the American Church.

Dresden, Saxony, *August* 19, 1869.

TO THE EDITOR OF "THE TIMES."

Sir,—Mr. Anketell, of Dresden, has ventured to assert that my statements regarding the state of religion in Germany are "strikingly inaccurate," though he has not condescended to point out one single inaccuracy into which I have fallen.

A five years' residence as British Chaplain in Dresden has taught me to distrust the value of first impressions. The longer I lived in Germany the more favourable views I was led to entertain of the state of religion there. Earnest preachers in Germany have usually as many and enthusiastic followers as similarly minded men have in England. The sermons of Dr. Langbein and of Dr. Rüling at Dresden are constantly attended by congregations averaging over two thousand. The same can be said of Dr. Meier's sermons at the Frauenkirche, and of others. The zealous pastoral work of Pastor Fröhlich in connexion with the Deaconesses' Institution is well known to those who seek acquaintance with such subjects; and very few indeed of the Dresden clergy are Rationalists.

There is a very considerable number of truly Christian people in Dresden, and although there is a large body of the people leavened with Rationalistic views, yet year by year that is becoming smaller. The Dresden clergy have awakened to the need of working among the masses, and the "Inner Mission" is now being actively carried on in Saxony. Several special Sunday services for children have been set on foot, and if people have only eyes to see, and know how to use them, they cannot deny that there are more than signs of an evangelical reaction. I can bear testimony to the piety, earnestness, and scholarship of many of the clergy, not only in Dresden and its environs, but also in Leipsic.

Some good men in Germany may naturally fear for the results if the connexion of Church and State were to be severed; but similar fears are expressed by good men in England. Mr. Anketell, too, as an American, cannot well understand the peculiar difficulties which lie sometimes in the way of a State clergy. The large size of parishes is often a serious hindrance to pastoral visitations, and there are no small difficulties in the way of altering this state of things. I can cite instances where the connexion with the State has seriously retarded evangelical action. I have no fears for the ultimate result if the State connexion were withdrawn. The earnest and aggressive Christian minority would soon gain ground upon the indifferent majority. Several of the Dresden clergy would work more energetically if their official position permitted them. Germany suffers much from the want of free Dissenting churches alongside of the State Church.

Germany, I emphatically repeat, has full right to be called a Christian land. I have learnt from intercourse with Christians there not to deny the possession of a living Christianity to Protestant brethren who may and do differ from many of my most cherished convictions. German Christians are not to be weighed by an English, or even an American, standard. I only hope Mr. Anketell may prove as zealous a Christian Minister as some of those whom he contemptuously styles "spiritual policemen or religious scavengers."

Yours very truly,
CHARLES H. H. WRIGHT, M.A.,

August 24, 1869.   Chaplain of Trinity Church, Boulogne.

TO THE EDITOR OF "THE TIMES."

Sir,—Since Mr. Wright, of Boulogne, complains that I have not specified the "inaccuracies" in his former letter, permit me to review some of the statements in his second.

1. "The sermons of Drs. Langbein and Rüling are attended by congregations of over two thousand."

The sermons of these eloquent divines are, as I know, largely attended; but the fact still remains that out of a Protestant population in Dresden of over one hundred and fifty thousand, only six thousand or seven thousand attend public worship on the Lord's Day. Where are the rest?

2. "Very few, indeed, of the Dresden clergy are Rationalists."

Last February I attended by invitation a gathering of the Protestant clergy of Dresden, where the subject of religious belief was discussed. The sentiments were broached that "Arius was as good a Christian as Athanasius," and "the Lord's Prayer is Creed enough for Christendom." All present, except, of course, myself, assented to these propositions. I am not sufficiently acquainted with Mr. Wright's theological opinions to know whether he would consider these views "Rationalistic" or not.

3. "There is a very considerable number of truly Christian people in Dresden."

This is certainly to be hoped and believed; but when Mr. Wright goes on and says,—

4. "The number of Rationalists is year by year becoming smaller,"

I can only say I differ from him in this opinion *toto cœlo*.

5. "The large size of parishes is often a serious hindrance to pastoral visitations."

This is what we would call in America "drawing it mild." Every candid observer must have noticed that pastoral visitations, as practised in England and America, are here almost unheard of. I remember when a student in Prussia, a dozen years ago, a brother student, son of a Lutheran clergyman, told me that pastoral visits were quite impossible, because, if attempted, they would be ascribed to licentious motives!* Another reason, whether cause or result, is, that the pastors are not received in the best society.

A parishioner of mine, who has resided here fifteen years (a former parishioner of Mr. Wright's, when he was chaplain here), has written on the subject :—

" The office of clergyman is never sought by the higher classes; these men are looked upon as a body belonging to the community, who are to preach sermons, baptize, marry, confirm, and administer the sacraments, all of which are matters of pounds, shillings, and pence. You barter whether you will have a first class wedding or a common one. If the former, the church produces velvet cushions; if the latter, straw-bottomed chairs. Your child must be christened when six weeks old—this is the law; a dollar a week can defer it at your pleasure. At the sacrament of the Lord's Supper each member brings his offering and lays it on the altar; this becomes the emolument of the priest (pastor), who quietly pockets it during the holy office. He is never expected to visit his parishioners. In fact, except in small country villages, no single clergyman, as

* The moral tone of German society renders this imputation simply absurd. [Author's note.]

with us, has a congregation he can call his own. There are, say, twenty in a large city, who preach in rotation in the different churches,* and, of course, the most eloquent are followed and have the largest audiences, as elsewhere. As there is no domestic intercourse between the clergyman and his people, his religious influence is confined to his pulpit."

The whole is well summed up in the remark that Luther may "have discovered the pearl of great price; but it has a wonderfully poor setting in his own land!" I cannot venture to trespass longer on your space, or I might cite the decision of the Dresden Protestant Verein last March, to the effect that the doctrine of Christ's atonement for human sin was an exploded superstition; and many other facts and evidences which I have been carefully collecting. But your Berlin correspondent has so faithfully portrayed the present religious aspect of Germany that I need not recite a twice-told tale, unless it is necessary for the information of Mr. Wright.

I have the honour to be, Sir, your faithful and obedient servant,

JOHN ANKETELL, A.M.,
Rector of St. John's (American) Church.
DRESDEN, *August* 27, 1869.

The word printed "resented" in my last letter should have read "treated."

* There are but very few German towns in which this is the case. [Author's note.]

TO THE EDITOR OF "THE TIMES."

Sir,—Though professing to answer and refute the statements made in my letter of the 24th ult., Mr. Anketell has left its main statements quite unanswered.

1. Although the state of religion in Germany is not satisfactory, I still maintain that there is a decided reaction in favour of evangelical truth. Mr. Anketell considerably underrates the number of persons who attend worship on the Lord's Day. It must be borne in mind that the number of Germans who attend church oftener than once a day is very small, so that the number attending church on any given Sunday would represent a greater number of persons than it would in England, where numbers attend church regularly twice a day. The number also of those who attend habitually every Sunday is much smaller than in England. Nearly one-third of the population at Dresden are at least occasional attendants at Divine service. The attendance at public worship now is much greater than twenty years ago, if the testimony I have received from Germans in Dresden is to be credited, and this improvement is due greatly to the earnestness and evangelical preaching of some of the clergy.

2. As I do not know which of the clergy attended the meeting Mr. Anketell alludes to, I cannot test the correctness of his statement nor attempt to qualify it. But from personal knowledge I assert that the majority of the Dresden clergy are Trinitarians. Drs. Liebner, Langbein, Rüling, Kohlschütter, Meier, and others are decidedly opposed to Rationalism, although they are not all of the High Lutheran party. I cannot think of more than some three

or four who would be likely to endorse such sentiments as Mr. Anketell refers to, unless those sentiments were considerably qualified by the context in which they occurred. I can scarcely credit Mr. Anketell's profession that he is not sufficiently acquainted with my theological opinions as to be able to say whether I am verging towards Rationalism or not, inasmuch as so many of his congregation have been attached members of my own. To prevent any person being so far misled by "M. A.'s" professed ignorance as to regard me as a sympathizer with Rationalism, permit me to state that my theological views harmonize in the main with those of the Evangelical party in the Church of England, as my published works are sufficient to prove to those unacquainted with my proceedings.

3. When I stated that there was a considerable number of truly Christian people in Dresden, I referred to the fact that among the educated German laity in Dresden were to be found not a few believers in the leading doctrines of the Christian faith.

4. Mr Anketell differs *toto cœlo* from my opinion that the number of Rationalists is decreasing every year. I think I can adduce as good reasons for holding my opinion as he can for holding his.

5. There is no question that in Dresden the enormous size of the parishes has prevented some earnest men from attempting pastoral visitations. In country places I have known German pastors equally active in this respect as English clergymen similarly situated. If the clergy had fewer official duties to perform, and smaller parishes were assigned them, there would soon be a marked improvement in this respect. English and American chaplains would

exercise much more influence for good if, instead of standing on some supposed superiority in themselves, or in their Church, and of abusing the clergy of the country in which they sojourn, they were to seek to hold fraternal intercourse with them, and to understand their peculiar positions and difficulties. We have much to learn from the German clergy, if we have something which we can impart to them in return.

6. In order not to extend the length of this too lengthy letter, I will not enter into the questions mooted in the quotation from the work of my lady friend referred to. As regards the class, however, from which the German clergy are drawn, I might remark it is the same as that from which the ranks of the Scottish clergy are generally recruited. One must remember that till very lately the army was the only profession into which the higher classes would enter. The position of the clergy in Germany is not inferior to that of the advocates and physicians in that land.

7. As to the Protestanten-Verein, it ought to be known that the members of that body are all decided Rationalists of an extreme type. That body has few sympathizers among the Saxon clergy, and its meetings are not generally attended by many of the better classes.

I must, in conclusion, profess my total ignorance of any edifice known as St. John's Church existing in Dresden. As Americans, however, do wonders, perhaps such a building has been erected during the last twelve months.

Yours very truly,

C. H. H. WRIGHT, M.A.,
Chaplain of Trinity Church, Boulogne.

B.—DOCUMENTS RELATING TO THE ŒCUMENICAL COUNCIL.

SYLLABUS ERRORUM.

"CATALOGUE EMBRACING THE PRINCIPAL ERRORS OF OUR TIME, AS INDICATED IN THE CONSISTORIAL ALLOCUTIONS, IN THE ENCYCLICALS, AND OTHER APOSTOLICAL LETTERS OF OUR MOST HOLY LORD POPE PIUS IX.

"Section I.—Pantheism, Naturalism, and Absolute Rationalism.

"1. There is no Highest, Most Wise, Most Providential, Divine Being as distinct from this universe, and God is the same with nature, and, therefore, subject to changes. God, in reality, takes his existence in man and the world, and all things are God, and have the veriest substance of God; and one and the same thing are God and the World, and hence also Spirit and Matter, Necessity and Liberty, the True and the False, the Just and Unjust. In effect, God is in man and in the world; and all things are God, and have the very substance of God. God is, therefore, one and the same thing with the world, and thence mind is confounded with matter, necessity with liberty of action, true with false, good with evil, just with unjust.—(All. '*Maxima quidem*,' June 9, 1862.)

"2. All action of God upon man and the world must be denied.—(All. '*Maxima quidem*,' June 9, 1862.)

"3. Human reason is, utterly without any regard to God,

the sole arbiter of true and false, good and evil; it is its own law for itself, and suffices by its natural powers to take care of the welfare of men and nations.—(All. '*Maxima quidem*,' June 9, 1862.)

"4. All the truths of religion are derived from the power inherent in human reason; hence reason is the highest norm by which man can and must arrive at the knowledge of all truths of every kind.—(Encyc. '*Qui pluribus*,' Nov. 9, 1846; and '*Singulari quidem*,' March 17, 1856; and All. '*Maxima quidem*,' June 9, 1862.)

"5. The Divine revelation is imperfect, and, therefore, subject to a continual and indefinite progress corresponding to the progress of human reason.—(Encyc. '*Qui pluribus*,' Nov. 9, 1846; and All. '*Maxima quidem*,' June 9, 1862.)

"6. The Christian faith is opposed to human reason, and the Divine revelation does not only not assist, but is even hurtful to the perfection of man.—(Encyc. '*Qui pluribus*,' Nov. 9, 1846, and All. '*Maxima quidem*,' June 9, 1862.)

"7. The prophecies and miracles told and narrated in Holy Scripture are fictions of poets, and the mysteries of the Christian faith an aggregate of philosophical investigations; and in the books of both Testaments there are found mythical inventions, fabulous fictions, and Jesus Christ himself is a mythical fiction.—(Encyc. '*Qui pluribus*,' Nov. 9, 1846; All. '*Maxima quidem*,' June 9, 1862.)

"Section II.—Moderate Rationalism.

"8. Since human reason is equal to religion itself, theological science must be treated like that of philosophy.— (All. '*Singulari quidem perfusi*.')

"9. All dogmas of the Christian religion are indiscriminately an object of natural science or philosophy, and human reason, if only historically cultivated, is able by its natural powers and principles to arrive at a real knowledge of all, even the most recondite, dogmas, so that these dogmas have been placed as an object before this same reason.—(Letter to Archbishop Freysing, '*Gravissimas,*' Dec. 4, 1862; letter to the same, '*Tuas libenter,*' Dec. 21, 1863.)

"10. As the philosopher is one thing and philosophy is another, it is the right and duty of the former to submit himself to the authority which he himself shall have recognized as true; but philosophy neither can nor ought to submit to any authority.—(Letter to Archbishop Freysing, '*Gravissimas,*' Dec. 11, 1862; letter to the same, '*Tuas libenter,*' Dec. 21, 1863.)

"11. The Church not only ought in no way to interfere with philosophy, but ought to tolerate even the errors of philosophy, leaving it to her to correct herself.—(Letter to Archbishop Freysing, '*Gravissimas,*' Dec. 11, 1862.)

"12. The decrees of the Apostolic See and of the Roman congregations fetter the free progress of science.—(Letter to Archbishop Freysing, '*Tuas libenter,*' Dec. 21, 1863.)

"13. The method and principles in which the old scholastic doctors have treated theology are in no way suitable to the demands of the age and the progress of sciences.—(Id. '*Tuas libenter,*' Dec. 21, 1863.)

"14. Philosophy must be studied, without any reference to supernatural revelation.—(Id., ibid.)

"N.B.—With the Rationalistic system are connected, in great part, the errors of Anton Günther, condemned in the letter to the Cardinal Archbishop of Cologne ('*Eximiam tuam,*' June 15, 1847), and in that to the Bishop of Breslau ('*Dolore haud mediocri,*' April 30, 1860).

"SECTION III.—INDIFFERENTISM—LATITUDINARIANISM.

"15. Every man is free to embrace and profess that religion which he, guided by the light of reason, believes to be the true one.—(Apostolic Letter, '*Multiplices inter,*' June 10, 1851; All. '*Maxima quidem,*' June 9, 1862.)

"16. Men may, in the observation of any religion, find and obtain eternal salvation.—(Encyc. '*Qui pluribus,*' Nov. 9, 1846; All. '*Ubi primum,*' Dec. 17, 1847; Encyc. '*Singulari quidem,*' March 17, 1856.)

"17. One should at least hope for the salvation of all those who are in no wise within the true Church of Christ. —(All. '*Singulari quâdam,*' Dec. 9, 1854; Encyc. '*Quanto conficiamur,*' Aug. 10, 1863.)

"18. Protestantism is nothing else than a different form of one and the same true Christian religion, in which it is as possible to please God as it is in the Catholic Church.— (Encyc. '*Noscitis et Nobiscum,*' Dec. 8, 1849.)

"SECTION IV.—SOCIALISM, COMMUNISM, SECRET SOCIETIES, BIBLICAL SOCIETIES, CLERICO-LIBERAL SOCIETIES.

"Pests of this description have been often and in the severest terms reproved,—in the Encyc. '*Qui pluribus,*' November 9, 1846; in the All. '*Quibus quantisque,*' April 20, 1849; in the Encyc. '*Noscitis et Nobiscum,*' December 8, 1849; in the All. '*Singulari quâdam,*' December 9, 1854; in the Encyc. '*Quanto conficiamur mœrore,*' August 10, 1863.

"SECTION V.—ERRORS RESPECTING THE CHURCH AND HER RIGHTS.

"19. The Church is not a true and perfect free society, nor does she rest upon her own and perpetual rights conferred upon her by her Divine founder; but it appertains to the civil power to define what are the rights and limits within which the Church may exercise these rights.—(All. '*Singulari quâdam*,' December 9, 1854; '*Multis gravibusque*,' December 17, 1860; '*Maxima quidem*,' June 9, 1862.)

"20. The ecclesiastical power must not exercise its authority without the permission and assent of the Civil Government.—(All. '*Meminit unusquisque*,' September 30, 1851.)

"21. The Church has not the power of defining dogmatically that the religion of the Catholic Church is, exclusively, the true religion.—(Apost. Let. '*Multiplices inter*,' June 10, 1851.)

"22. The obligation whereby Catholic teachers and writers are absolutely bound is limited to those matters only which are represented by the infallible judgment of the Church as dogmas to be believed in by all.—(Letter to Archbishop Freysing, '*Tuas libenter*,' December 21, 1863.)

"23. The Roman pontiffs and Œcumenical Councils have exceeded the limits of their power, have usurped rights of Sovereigns, and have also committed errors in defining matters of dogma and morals.—(Apost. Let. '*Multiplices inter*,' June 10, 1851.)

"24. The Church has not the power to use force, nor has she any direct or indirect temporal power.—(Apost. Let. '*Ad Apostolicæ*,' August 22, 1851.)

"25. Besides the authority inherent in the Episcopate, another temporal power is granted to it by the civil power either expressly or tacitly, but therefore also revocable by the civil power whenever it pleases.—(Apost. Let. '*Ad Apostolicæ*,' August 22, 1851.)

"26. The Church has not any natural and legitimate right of acquiring and possessing.—('*Nunquam*,' December 18, 1856; Encyc. '*Incredibili*,' September 17, 1868.)

"27. The Holy Ministers of the Church and the Roman Pontiff ought to be absolutely excluded from all charge and dominion over temporal affairs.—(All. '*Maxima quidem*,' June 9, 1862.)

"28. Bishops have not the right of promulgating even apostolical letters without the sanction of the Government. —(All. '*Nunquam fore*,' December 15, 1856.)

"29. Spiritual graces granted by the Roman Pontiff must be considered null unless they have been asked for by the civil Government.—(Id., ibid.)

"30. The immunity of the Church and of ecclesiastical persons had derived its origin from civil law.—(Apost. Let. '*Multiplices inter*,' June 10, 1851.)

"31. The Ecclesiastical jurisdiction for temporal lawsuits, whether civil or criminal, of the clergy, is to be utterly abolished, even without asking and notwithstanding the protest of the holy See.—(All. '*Acerbissimum*,' September 27, 1852; id. '*Nunquam fore*,' December 15, 1856.)

"32. Without any violation of natural right or equity,

the personal immunity whereby the clergy are exempt from performing military duties, may be abrogated, this abrogation being called for by civil progress, especially in a commonwealth constituted upon principles of liberal government.—(Let. to Bishop Montisregal, '*Singularis nobilisque*,' September 29, 1864.)

"33. It does not appertain exclusively to ecclesiastical jurisdiction by any proper and inherent right to direct the doctrine in theological matters.—(Letter to Archbishop Freysing, '*Tuas libenter*,' December 21, 1863.)

"34. The doctrine of those who compare the Roman Pontiff to a free Sovereign acting in the Universal Church is a doctrine which prevailed in the Middle Ages.—(Apost. Let. '*Ad Apostolicæ*,' August 22, 1851.)

"35. There is no obstacle to the sentence of a General Council or the act of all nations transferring the Papal Sovereignty from the Bishopric and city of Rome to some other bishop in another city.—(Id., ibid.)

"36. The definition of a National Council does not admit of any other discussion, and the civil power may act in conformity with this.—(Id., ibid.)

"37. National Churches may be established without the authority of and totally separated from the Roman Pontiff. —(All. '*Multis gravibusque*,' December 17, 1860; '*Jamdudum cernimus*,' March 18, 1861.)

"38. The too arbitrary bearing of the Roman Pontiffs has contributed to the division of the Church into Eastern and Western.—(Apost. Let. '*Ad Apostolicæ*,' August 22, 1851.)

"Section VI.—Errors of Civil Society as much by itself as considered in its relations to the Church.

"39. The State, as the origin and source of all rights, possesses a certain right not circumscribed by any limit.— (All. '*Maxima quidem*,' June 9, 1862.)

"40. The doctrine of the Catholic Church is opposed to the laws and interests of human society.—(Encyc. '*Qui pluribus*,' November 9, 1846; All. '*Quibus quantisque*,' April 20, 1849.)

"41. To the civil power, even when exercised by an infidel Sovereign, belongs an indirect and negative power over religious affairs; and, therefore, not only the law called 'Exequatur,' but also the so-called 'Jus appellationis ab abusu' is vested in it.—(Apost. Let., August 22, 1851.)

"42. In a legal conflict between the two powers the civil law prevails.—(Id., ibid.)

"43. The lay power has authority to rescind, to declare and render null, solemn Conventions (commonly called Concordats) entered into with regard to rights belonging to ecclesiastical immunity with the Holy See, without the consent of the same, and even notwithstanding its protest. —(All. '*In Consistoriali*,' November 1, 1850; '*Multis gravibusque*,' December 17, 1860.)

"44. The civil authority may interfere in matters relating to religion, morals, and spiritual government. Hence it has control over the instructions for the guidance of consciences issued, conformably with their office, by the pastors of the Church. Nay, it may decide even on the administration of the Divine Sacraments and the necessary arrangements for their reception.—(All. '*In Consistoriali*,' November 1, 1858; All. '*Maxima quidem*,' June 9, 1862.)

"45. The entire direction of public schools in which the youth of any Christian States are educated, except in some respects episcopal seminaries, may and must appertain to the civil authority, and belong to it in such a manner that no right shall be recognized as belonging to any other authority whatsoever of interfering in the discipline of the schools, in the direction of the studies, in the bestowing of degrees, or the choice and approval of the teachers.—(All. '*In consistoriali*,' November 1, 1850; '*Quibus luctuosissimis*,' September 5, 1851.)

"46. Even in clerical seminaries, the plan to be followed in the studies is to be submitted to the civil authority.—(All '*Nunquam fore*,' December 15, 1856.)

"47. The best arrangement of civil society requires that popular schools which are open to all children of the people without distinction, and public institutions destined to teach higher letters and discipline to the young, and to impart to them education, should be freed from all ecclesiastical authority and interference, and should be fully subjected to the civil and political authority, according to the pleasure of those in authority, in accordance with the common opinions of the times.—(Letter to Archbishop Freyburg, '*Quum non sine*,' July 14, 1864.)

"48. This manner of instructing youth, alienated from the Catholic faith and from the power of the Church, and which teaches the science of natural things and the objects of terrestrial social life, either exclusively, or at least in the first instance, may be approved by Catholics.—(Id., ibid.)

"49. The civil power is entitled to prevent ministers of religion and faithful nations from communicating freely and mutually with the Roman Pontiff.—(All. '*Maxima quidem*,' June 9, 1862.)

"50. The lay authority possesses of itself the right of presenting bishops, and may require of them that they take possession of their dioceses before having received canonical institution and the apostolical letter from the Holy See.— (All. '*Nunquam fore*,' December 15, 1856.)

"51. The lay authority has even the right of deposing bishops from the exercise of their pastoral functions, and is not bound to obey the Roman Pontiff in matters affecting the founding of sees and the institution of bishops.—(Apost. Let. '*Multiplices inter*,' June 10, 1851; All. '*Acerbissimum*,' September 27, 1852.)

"52. The Government may by its own authority alter the period fixed by the Church for the taking of conventual vows by both sexes, and may enjoin upon all religious establishments to admit nobody to the solemn vows without its permission.—(All. '*Nunquam fore*,' December 15, 1856.)

"53. Laws respecting the protection, rights, and functions of religious establishments must be abrogated; nay, the civil Government may lend its assistance to all those who desire to abandon the religious life chosen and to break their solemn vows. The Government may in the same way abolish religious establishments as well as collegial churches and simple benefices, even when subject to the right of the Patronate, and may place their goods and revenues under the administration and disposition of the civil power.— (All. '*Acerbissimum*,' September 27, 1862; '*Probe meministis*,' January 22, 1855; and '*Quum sæpe*,' July 26, 1858.)

" 54. Kings and princes are not only free from the jurisdiction of the Church, but are even superior to the Church in the litigation questions of jurisdiction.—(Apost. Let. '*Multiplices inter*,' June 10, 1851.)

" 55. The Church ought to be separated from the State, and the State from the Church.—(All. '*Acerbissimum*,' September 27, 1862.)

" SECTION VII.—ERRORS IN NATURAL AND CHRISTIAN MORALS.

" 56. Moral laws do not stand in need of the Divine sanction, and there is not the least necessity that human laws should be conformable to the law of nature or should receive their binding power from God.—(All. '*Maxima quidem*,' June 9, 1862.)

" 57. The science of philosophy and morals as well as the civil laws can and must be independent from Divine and ecclesiastical authority.—(Id., ibid.)

" 58. No other powers are to be recognized than those which inhere in matter, and all moral discipline and honesty is to be placed in the accumulation and increase of riches by every means, and in the satisfaction of lust.—(Id., ibid. All. '*Maxima quidem;*' Encyc. '*Quanto conficiamur*,' August 10, 1863.)

" 59. Right consists in the material facts, and all human duties are vain words, and all human facts have the force of right.—(All. '*Maxima quidem*,' June 9, 1862.)

" 60. Authority is nothing but the sum of numbers and material forces.—(Id., ibid.)

" 61. The injustice of a successful fact is not detrimental

to the sanctity of right.—(All. '*Jamdudum cernimus*,' March 18, 1861.)

"62. The so-called principle of non-intervention must be proclaimed and observed.—(All. '*Novos et ante*,' September 27, 1860.)

"63. It is allowable to refuse obedience to legitimate princes, and to rise in insurrection against them.—(Encyc. '*Qui pluribus*,' November 9, 1846; All. '*Quisque vestrum*,' October 4, 1847; Encyc. '*Noscitis et Nobiscum*,' December 8, 1849; Apost. Let. '*Cum Catholica*,' March 25, 1860.)

"64. Both the violation of any oath, even the most solemn, and even every guilty and shameful act repugnant to the eternal law, are not only not to be rebuked, but even allowable in every way and worthy of the highest praise when done from love of the country.—(All. '*Quibus quantisque*,' April 20, 1849.)

"SECTION VIII.—ERRORS AS TO CHRISTIAN MARRIAGE.

"65. It is in no way admissible that Christ has raised marriage to the dignity of a sacrament.—(Apost. Let. '*Ad Apostolicæ*,' August 22, 1852.)

"66. The sacrament of marriage is nothing but an adjunct to the contract, and separable from it, and the sacrament itself consists only in the nuptial benediction.— (Id., ibid.)

"67. By the law of nature the marriage tie is not indissoluble, and in many cases divorce, properly so called, may be pronounced by the civil authority.—(Id., ibid.; All. '*Acerbissimum*,' September 27, 1852.)

"68. The Church has no power of fixing impediments to

marriage; but to civil society belongs that power by which the existing hindrances can be removed.—(Apost. Let. '*Multiplices inter*,' June 10, 1851.)

"69. It is only in more recent centuries that the Church has begun to fix invalidating obstacles to marriage, availing herself, not of her own right, but of a right borrowed from the civil power.—(Apost. Let. '*Ad Apostolicæ*,' August 22, 1851.)

"70. The Canons of the Council of Trent which pronounce the censure of anathema against those who dare to deny the Church the right of fixing invalidating obstacles are either not dogmatic, or to be considered as emanating from borrowed power.—(Id., ibid.)

"71. The Tridentine form does not, under penalty of nullity, bind in cases where the civil law has appointed another form, and desires that this new form is to be used in marriage.—(Id., ibid.)

"72. Boniface VIII. was the first who declared that the vow of chastity pronounced at ordination annuls nuptials.—(Id., ibid.)

"73. By the power of a mere civil contract a marriage, in the true sense of the word, may well exist between Christians, and it is false either that the marriage contract between Christians must either always be a sacrament, or that the contract is null if the sacrament is excluded.—(Id., ibid., Letter of Pius IX. to King of Sardinia, September 9, 1852; All. '*Acerbissimum*,' September 27, 1852; '*Multis gravibusque*,' December 17, 1860.)

"74. Matrimonial or nuptial causes belong by their nature to civil jurisdiction.—(Apost. Let. '*Ad Apostolicæ*,' August 22, 1851; All. '*Acerbissimum*,' September 27, 1852.)

"N.B. To this place belong also two other errors regarding the abolition of the celibacy of priests, and the preference due to the state of marriage over that of virginity. The errors condemned have been refuted: the first in Encyc. '*Qui pluribus*,' November 9, 1846; the second in Apost. Let. '*Multiplices inter*,' June 10, 1851.)

"SECTION IX.—ERRORS REGARDING THE CIVIL POWER OF THE SOVEREIGN PONTIFF.

"75. The sons of the Christian-Catholic Church are not agreed upon the compatibility of the temporal with the spiritual power.—(Apost. Let. '*Ad Apostolicæ*,' August 22, 1852.)

"76. The abrogation of the temporal power possessed by the Apostolic See would contribute to the happiness and liberty of the Church.—(All. '*Quibus quantisque*,' April 20, 1849.)

"N.B. Besides these errors, explicitly pointed out, still several others are condemned by implication by the proposition and assertion of the doctrine which all Catholics are bound to respect touching the temporal Government of the Sovereign Pontiff. These doctrines are lucidly explained in All. '*Quibus quantisque*,' April 20, 1849; in All. '*Si semper antea*,' May 20, 1850; Apost. Let. '*Quum Catholica Ecclesia*,' March 26, 1860; All. '*Novos*,' September 28, 1860; '*Jamdudum*,' March 18, 1861; and '*Maxima quidem*,' June 9, 1862.)

"SECTION X.—ERRORS REFERRING TO MODERN LIBERALISM.

"77. In these our days it is no longer expedient that the Catholic religion shall be held as the only religion of the State, to the exclusion of all other creeds.—(All. '*Nemo vestrûm*,' July 26, 1855.)

"78. Hence it has laudably been ordained by the law in some countries called Catholic that emigrants shall enjoy the free exercise of their own individual worship, whatever it be.—(All. '*Acerbissimum*,' September 27, 1852.)

"79. For it is false that the civil liberty of every mode of worship and the full power given to all of openly and publicly displaying their opinions and their thoughts conduces to corrupt the morals and minds of the people more easily, and to the propagation of the pest of indifference.—All. '*Nunquam fore*,' December 15, 1856.)

"80. The Roman Pontiff can and ought to reconcile himself to and to come to an understanding with progress, liberalism, and modern civilization.—(All. '*Jamdudum cernimus*,' March 18, 1861.)"

THE TWENTY-ONE CANONS:

BEING THE

DRAFT OF A DOGMATICAL DECREE ON THE CHURCH OF CHRIST, BASED UPON THE SYLLABUS, AND SUBMITTED TO THE ŒCUMENICAL COUNCIL BY THE POPE IN FEBRUARY, 1870.

Canon 1. If any man say that the religion of Christ does not exist, and is not expressed, in any particular association instituted by Christ himself, but that it may be properly observed and exercised by individuals separately without relation to any society which may be the true Church of Christ, let him be anathema.

2. If any man say that the Church has not received from the Lord Jesus Christ any certain and immutable form of constitution, but that, like other human associations, it has been subject, and may be subject, according to the changes of times, to vicissitudes and variations, let him be anathema.

3. If any man say that the Church of the divine promises is not an external and visible society, but is entirely internal and invisible, let him be anathema.

4. If any man say that the true Church is not a body one in itself, but that it is composed of various and dispersed Societies bearing the Christian title, and that it is common to them all, or that various societies differing from each

other in profession of faith and holding separate communion, constitute, as members and portions, a Church of Christ one and universal, let him be anathema.

5. If any man say, that the Church of Christ is not a society absolutely necessary for eternal salvation, or that men may be saved by the adoption of any other religion whatsoever, let him be anathema.

6. If any man say that this intolerance whereby the Catholic Church proscribes and condemns all religious sects which are separate from her communion, is not prescribed by the Divine law, or that with respect to the truth of religion it is possible to have opinions only, but not certainty, and that, consequently, all religious sects should be tolerated by the Church, let him be anathema.

7. If any man say, that the same Church of Christ may be obscured by darkness, or infected with evils, in consequence of which it may depart from the wholesome truth of the faith and manners, deviate from its original institution, or terminate only in becoming corrupt and depraved, let him be anathema.

8. If any man say, that the present Church of Christ is not the last and supreme institution for obtaining salvation, but that another is to be looked for from a new and fuller outpouring of the Holy Spirit, let him be anathema.

9. If any man say, that the Infallibility of the Church is restricted solely to things which are contained in Divine revelation, and that it does not also extend to other truths, which are necessary in order that the great gift of revelation may be preserved in its integrity, let him be anathema.

10. If any man say, that the Church is not a perfect society, but a corporation (*collegium*), or that as such in

respect of civil society or the State it is subject to secular domination, let him be anathema.

11. If any man say, that the Church divinely instituted is like to a society of equals ; that the Bishops have indeed an office and a ministry, but not a power of governing proper to themselves which is bestowed upon them by Divine ordination, and which they ought to exercise freely, let him be anathema.

12. If any man hold that Christ, our Lord and Sovereign, has only conferred upon his Church a directing power by means of its counsels and persuasions, but not of ordering by its laws, or of constraining and compelling by antecedent judgments and salutary penalties those who wander and those who are contumacious, let him be anathema.

13. If any man say, that the true Church of Christ, out of which no one can be saved, is any other than the Holy Roman Catholic and Apostolic Church, let him be anathema.

14. If any man say, that the Apostle St. Peter has not been instituted by our Lord Christ as Prince of all the Apostles and visible Head of the Church Militant, or that he received only the preeminence of honour, but not the primacy of sole and true jurisdiction, let him be anathema.

15. If any man say, that it does not follow from the institution of our Lord Christ himself that St. Peter has perpetual successors in his Primacy over the Universal Church or that the Roman Pontiff is not by Divine right the successor of Peter in that same primacy, let him be anathema.

16. If any man say, that the Roman Pontiff has only a function of inspection and direction, but not a full and

supreme power of jurisdiction over the Universal Church, or that his power is not ordinary and immediate over the whole Church, taken as a whole or separately, let him be anathema.

17. If any man say, that the independent ecclesiastical power respecting which the Church teaches that it has been conferred upon it by Christ, and the supreme civil power cannot co-exist, so that the rights of each may be observed, let him be anathema.

18. If any man say that the power which is necessary for the government of civil society, does not emanate from God, or that no obedience is due to it by virtue even of the law of God, or that such power is repugnant to the natural liberty of man, let him be anathema.

19. If any man say that all rights existing among men are derived from the political State, or that there is no authority besides that which is communicated by such State, let him be anathema.

20. If any man say that in the law of the political State, or in the public opinion of men has been deposited the Supreme Rule of conscience for public and social actions, or that the judgments by which the Church pronounces upon what is lawful and what is unlawful, do not extend to such actions, or that by the force of civil law an act, which by virtue of Divine or ecclesiastical law is unlawful, can become lawful, let him be anathema.

21. If any man say that the laws of the Church have no binding force until they have been confirmed by the sanction of the civil power, or that it belongs to the said civil power to judge and to decree in matters of religion by virtue of its supreme authority, let him be anathema.

THE INFALLIBILITY BILL,

AS PROPOSED BY THE POPE TO THE ŒCUMENICAL COUNCIL ON MARCH 6, 1870.

LATIN ORIGINAL.

I.—BILL.

Caput addendum decreto de Romani Pontificis Primatu. Romanum Pontificem in rebus fidei et morum definiendis errare non posse.

Sancta Romana ecclesia summum et plenum primatum et principatum super universam catholicam ecclesiam obtinet, quem se ab ipso domino in beato Petro, apostolorum principe, cujus Romanus Pontifex est successor, cum potestatis plenitudine recepisse veraciter et humiliter recognoscit. Et sicuti præ cæteris tenetur fidei veritatem defendere, sic et si quæ de fide subortæ fuerint quæstiones suo debent iudicio definiri.* Et quia non potest domini nostri Jesu Christi prætermitti sententia dicentis: "tu es Petrus, et super hanc petram ædificabo ecclesiam meam,"† hæc quæ dicta sunt rerum probantur effectibus, quia in sede apostolica immaculata est semper catholica servata religio et sancta celebrata doctrina: ‡ hinc sacro approbante concilio docemus et

* Ex professione fidei edita a Græcis in Conc. œc. Lugdun. II.
† Math. xvi. 18.
‡ Ex formula S. Hormisdæ Papæ subscripta a Patribus Conc. œc. VIII. Constantinop. IV.

tamquam fidei dogma definimus per divinam assistentiam fieri, ut Romanus Pontifex, qui in persona beati Petri dictum est ab eodem domino nostro Jesu Christo: "ego pro te rogavi ut non deficiat fides tua,"* cum supremi omnium Christianorum doctoris munere fungens pro auctoritate definit quid in rebus fidei et morum ab universa ecclesia tenendum sit, errare non possit; et hanc Romani Pontificis inerrantiae seu infallibilitatis praerogativam ad idem objectum porrigi, ad quod infallibilitas ecclesiae extenditur.

Si quis autem huic nostrae definitioni contradicere, quod Deus avertat, praesumpserit, sciat se a veritate fidei catholicae et ab unitate ecclesiae defecisse.

II.—Papal Message to the Council concerning the Bill.

Cum plurimi Episcopi petierint a Sanctissimo Domino Nostro, ut Concilio proponatur thema de infallibilitate Romani Pontificis, idemque Sanctissimus Dominus Noster, de consilio peculiaris Congregationis pro recipiendis et expendendis Patrum propositionibus deputatae, memoratae petitioni annuere dignatus sit; idcirco Rmis. Concilii Patribus examinanda distribuitur formula novi capitis ea de re agentis: quae formula schemati Constitutionis Dogmaticae *de Ecclesia Christi* inserenda erit post caput undecimum. Simul autem Rmi. P. P. monentur ut ii quibus super eodem capite undecimo et super praedicta formula, nec non super canonibus 14, 15, 16 aliquid observandum videbitur, animadversiones suas scripto tradant Secretario Concilii intra

* Luc. 22, 32.

decem dies, nempe a die octava usque ad diem decimam septimam Martii inclusive iuxta Decretum 20 Februarii proxime elapsi.

Ex Secretario Concilii Vaticani die 6 Martii 1870. Josephus Ep. S. Hippolyti Secretar. Concilii Vatic.

ENGLISH TRANSLATION.

I.—BILL.

" Chapter to be added to the Decree upon the Primacy of the Roman Pontiff, to the effect that the Roman Pontiff cannot err in the definition of matters of faith or morals.

" The Holy Roman Church possesses the supreme and complete primacy and principality over the Universal Catholic Church, which it verily and humbly acknowledges to have received with the plenitude of the power of the Lord himself in the person of St. Peter, the Prince of Apostles, of whom the Roman Pontiff is the successor.

" And as, above all things, it behoves it to make clear the truth of the faith, all questions which may arise upon matters of faith must be determined by its judgment, seeing that otherwise the words of the Lord Jesus Christ (Thou art Peter and upon this rock will I build my Church) would be disregarded.

" That which has been set forth upon this point has been proved by the results, as in the Apostolic See the Catholic religion has always been preserved immaculate, and its doctrine has always been maintained at its fulness.

" Consequently, we inculcate, with the concurrence of the Holy Council, and we define as a dogma of faith, that, thanks to the Divine assistance, it is that the Roman Pontiff, of whom it was said in the person of St. Peter by our same Lord Jesus Christ, " I have prayed for thee, that thy faith fail not, and when thou art converted, strengthen thy brethren," cannot err when, acting in his quality as supreme teacher of all Christians, he defines what the Universal Church must hold in matters of faith and morals, and that the prerogative of inerrancy or infallibility extends over the same matters to which the infallibility of the Church is applicable. But if any one should dare—which may God forbid!—to controvert our present definition, let him know that he departs from the truth of the faith."

II.—PAPAL MESSAGE TO THE COUNCIL CONCERNING THE BILL.

SECRETARIAT OF THE VATICAN COUNCIL,
March 6, 1870.

As so many Bishops have beseeched our Most Sacred Master to submit to the Council a draft concerning the Infallibility of the Roman Pontiff, and as our Most Sacred Master, after consulting the Special Congregation appointed to receive and examine the propositions of the Fathers, has condescended to comply with the said request: for this reason the draft of a new chapter on this subject, to be inserted into the draft of the Dogmatical Decree on the Church of Christ after the eleventh chapter, is distributed among the Roman Fathers of the Council, that they may examine it. At the same time, those Roman Fathers who should wish to offer any remarks on the eleventh chapter, or on the new draft and the 14th, 15th, and 16th Canons, are, in accordance with the Decree of the 20th February, desired to transmit their remarks in writing to the Secretary of the Council in the ten days from March 8 to March 17.

JOSEPHUS EPISC. S. HIPPOLYTI,

Secretary to the Vatican Council.

The Roman correspondent of 'The Times' thus expresses himself on the above stupendous document:—

"In the document before me there are not a few assumptions. It is assumed that Jesus Christ gave to Peter supreme and full primacy and principality over the Universal Catholic Church. It is assumed, further, that in so doing He also gave it to the Holy Roman Church. It is assumed that the Roman Pontiff is the successor of Peter; and in that assumption is included the assumption that Peter was at Rome, and that he was Bishop of Rome— points upon which Scripture happens to be silent. It is assumed that whatever power Peter had, the Pontiff has from him, and this assumption is made "truly and humbly," for indeed the Pontiff cannot but be all truth and humility. It is assumed that the Roman Church is under a distinct obligation, and has a special power and authority for the definition; that is, for the absolute stopping of all questions of faith that may arise. This is to be done by "*its own*" judgment; that is, by the judgment of the Church of Rome. It is assumed that the words "Thou art Peter," &c., mean that the Church was to be built in Peter, not only as respects his character, his utterances, and his career, and as a prominent example of others like him, but also on the ground that he was the recognized chief of the Apostles and the predestined founder of a like succession. It is assumed that these words of our Lord addressed to Peter are proved to possess the particular significance ascribed to them by the Church of Rome by the test of results, those results being the singular and absolute immunity from doctrinal error enjoyed by the Apostolic See, which, it is assumed, has kept the whole faith, and that without spot, in a singular and remarkable manner. It is assumed that it is the place of the Pope to define—that is, to make and proclaim—articles of faith; and of an Œcumenical Council to approve. It is assumed that when our Lord said he had prayed for Peter that his faith should not fail, that prayer implied a promise that both Peter himself and his alleged successors the Bishops of Rome, would always have a perfectly right judgment in all theological, spiritual, moral, political, and social questions. . On these assumptions it is argued and concluded that the Roman Pontiff whenever he acts and speaks with authority—that is, in a formal and customary manner, according to rule and precedent—possesses and exhibits all the infallibility promised in Holy Writ to the whole Church; and that as far as the Church is infallible, so is he; in whatever matter it is infallible, in that matter is he."

And whoever does not believe in it all, will be accursed in this world and the next!

COUNT DARU'S LETTERS ON THE ŒCUMENICAL COUNCIL.

In the beginning of this year Count Daru, the French Minister of Foreign Affairs, wrote some letters to a person of high standing at Rome, in which he complained of the imprudence of the Pope, and threatened to withdraw the French garrison from the Holy City were Infallibility proclaimed as a dogma of the Church. The following are extracts from these important letters:—

"PARIS, 18 *Janvier*, 1870.

". . . J'ai vu avec regrets quelques unes des choses qui se sont passées, et cependant je ne peux pas croire à de trop grandes imprudences de la part de la Cour de Rome. On ne peut pas s'y aveugler assez pour supposer que le maintien de nos troupes serait possible le lendemain du jour où le dogme de l'Infallibilité serait prononcé. Nous voudrions les laisser à Rome que nous ne le pourrions pas. Il y aura un mouvement irrésistible de l'opinion en France, auquel il ne sera pas possible de ne pas céder.

"Certainement, le Saint Père le sait, le voit, le croit. Il se rendra, je l'espère, aux conseils plus modérés des plus illustres membres de l'Eglise de France.

"Recevez, &c.,
"DARU."

"Paris, 5 *Février*, 1870.

"Je vous remercie, Monsieur, des renseignements que vous voulez bien me donner. Je crains que le parti en majorité dans le Concile ne veuille abuser de ses avantages, et qu'il n'aille avec emportement vers le but. Les passions religieuses sont encore plus difficile à manier que les passions politiques.

"J'honore beaucoup la résistance que leur oppose la ferme attitude de la minorité des Évêques, et je la seconde de tous mes efforts. J'ai envoyé à plusieurs reprises les instructions du Gouvernement à M. de Banneville, qui me tient au courant de tout, et par sa bouche j'ai fait entendre la vérité au Cardinal Antonelli. Il est bien évident que tout peut être remis en question par la conduite des Prélats Italiens, Espagnoles, Missionaires, et Vicaires Apostoliques, qui semblent vivre dans un monde à part.

"Il est bien évident que l'on peut nous rendre impossible le maintien de notre garnison à Rome aussi bien que l'arrangement des affaires financières du Saint Siège, dont j'étais si bien disposé à m'occuper, que l'on peut infirmer gravement les engagements Concordataires, dont la Propagande ne parait pas tenir le moindre compte, et briser le pacte qui nous unit. J'en ai prévenu le Cardinal; je ne cesserai pas de lui représenter le danger de la position dans laquelle il se place, et il nous place; mais je ne suis pas sûr que ces représentations soient écoutées; on ne raisonne pas, on se laisse entraîner aux ardeurs du moment. Si la minorité peut gagner du temps, elle fera ce qu'il y a de mieux à faire dans ce moment-ci.

"Le parti révolutionnaire qui se remue depuis quelque temps nous donne ici un peu d'embarras.

"Il conspire et semble vouloir agir prochainement. Combien on est aveugle à Rome, si l'on ne s'aperçoit pas qu'on lui donne des armes, que là est le danger ; que briser la force conservative en face d'un tel péril est un acte insensé ! que compromettre la religion par des Syllabus, c'est jouer le jeu de ceux qui l'attaquent audacieusement tous les jours à visage découvert, dans leurs paroles comme dans leurs écrits ! Je crois que les complots révolutionnaires ne réussiront pas, et que ses tentatives seront reprimés, mais ils sont un symptôme de l'état des esprits, et l'on devrait en tenir quelque compte à Rome.

"Recevez, &c.,

"Daru."

COUNT DARU'S MEMORANDUM ON THE COUNCIL.

TOWARDS the end of March Count Daru, the then French Minister of Foreign Affairs, caused a Memorandum to be drawn up against the proceedings of the Council. It officially reiterated the warnings previously addressed to the Pope in a less authoritative form. But M. Ollivier, the French Prime Minister, objected to these energetic politics of his colleague. In his opinion, to blame the Pope was a dangerous game to play on the eve of a *plébiscite*. It might lose him the goodwill of the rural priesthood, without which the requisite number of votes could not be got together for Napoleon III. It might spoil the demonstrative expression of popular confidence in the Emperor, so carefully prepared by the Cabinet. Count Daru resigned. His Memorandum, as it could not be entirely withdrawn, having already obtained the approval of some other Courts, was subsequently communicated at Rome semi-demi-officially, and on the distinct understanding that it would not be acted upon. The following are the most important passages of this remarkable documemt :—

" Recently, questions of political and State interest have been mooted in the Council. The relations between the Church and the State have been the subject of propositions which are soon to be brought under discussion. His Majesty's Government has, therefore, felt it a right and a duty to offer some observations upon this special point, and to indicate the inconveniences which may follow upon the adoption of maxims which trench upon the laws of the country. In the exercise of this right, and for the accomplishment of this duty, it does not apply any pressure that can in any degree trammel the deliberations of the august Council. Its intervention is purely moral, and it is confined to matters which are indisputably within the category of civil power. In requiring that the laws and rights of civil society should be respected, it is careful to avoid even the semblance of disrespect towards the rights and liberties of religious society. It intervenes simply because it appears to it that the limits between the separate domains have been exceeded. Confiding, respectful, fixed in our sentiments, we address ourselves to the generous mind of the Holy Father; we recall to his recollection those relations of mutual good will which, during seventy years, have united the two Governments, and have insured social and religious peace. It is in order to preserve those good relations that we urgently request from the wisdom of the Holy Pontiff and the Fathers of the Council to erase from the *Schema de Ecclesia* all those portions which in the text published, and not disavowed, would, we fear, have the gravest consequences to legal and social order in all the States of Europe. The more the doctrine embodied in that document is examined, the more apparent is it that this doctrine substantially involves a complete subordination of civil society to religious society. We wish that plausible explanations or desirable modifications could enable us to give to these resolutions a different interpretation. But in the present position of affairs, unless we refuse to give to words their real and natural meaning, it is impossible not to be convinced that the *Schema de Ecclesia* would have the object and end of re-establishing throughout the world the ascendancy of doctrines subordinating civil society to the rule of the clergy. In fact, according to the provisions contained in this *Schema*, and under the irresistible sanction of anathema, the infallibility and authority of the Church must extend not only to truths transmitted by revelation, but also to all those which may appear to be necessary to protect the records of tradition. In other words, this infallibility and this authority have no other limits than those assigned by the Church, and all principles of order—civil, political, scientific—fall directly or indirectly within their competence. It is in this almost boundless field that the right of the Church would be exercised to announce decisions and promulgate laws binding upon the consciences of the faithful, independently of any confirmation from political authority, and even in direct opposition to laws emanating from political authority. It is within this domain, the bounds of which the Church alone would seem to have power to define, that the Canons confer upon it complete power, at once legislative, judicial, and coercive, applicable to external acts as well as to internal impressions —a power which the Church would be enabled to enforce by material penalties, and to which Christian Princes and Governments would be bound to render their aid by punishing those who sought to evade them. It is evident that if such principles were applied in practice, if Governments were to retain no power, and civil societies no liberty, beyond the power and the liberty which it might please the Church to permit them, their most essential rights, the foundation of their political constitutions, the bases of their civil legislation in matters of property, family, and education, might at any time be brought in question by the ecclesiastical authority. As a complement of this system it has been proposed to include in the same decree the personal and separate Infallibility of the Pope—that is to say, after having concentrated all political and religious powers in the hands of the Church, to concentrate all the powers of the Church in the hands of its chief. Such are the measures which the Œcumenical Council would be called upon to proclaim in the nineteenth century; and as these maxims are not admitted or recognized in any part of Christian Europe, an universal anathema would be hurled in the name of the Holy Father against all institutions and all societies. We are told certainly that the Church declares abstract truths, but does not exact their application; that, if these doctrines conflict with existing laws, they conflict only in point of principle; in fact, they accommodate themselves to all forms of government and all legislations. Such a declaration is insufficient to reassure us. Can it be admitted that to-morrow, in the forty thousand parishes of France, it shall be taught that men are free to believe that they may think in one manner and act in another? This distinction would inflict upon tender consciences the most cruel torture. We have too much respect for the Church, we have too high an opinion of its power to allow such an argument. We are convinced that it is performing and will perform a serious task, and that, consequently, it will ever strive to reduce to practice those maxims which it has included in articles of belief as immutable verities. We could not admit that the most venerable of Pontiffs has gathered around his throne all the Bishops of the Catholic world simply to prepare and proclaim fruitless laws, to pass vain resolutions. It is added that these maxims are not new, that they simply reproduce the dogmas of an ancient theological teaching, and that the world has no reason to be astonished at them, since the Church has ever held the same language. We acknowledge that fact. It is not now for the first time that these doctrines make their appearance. They have been proclaimed in former ages and on various occasions. But all history attests that they have never been accepted in this form, and as a whole, by any Sovereign or by any nation, even in the times when the Catholic faith was universally held. At all times and in all countries the absolute independence of the temporal Government and the Sovereign authority has been emphatically insisted upon by peoples, by kings, and often by a national clergy. Even in the middle ages the attempt to enforce these principles was the occasion of the most sanguinary conflicts. The long struggle of the priesthood and the Germanic Empire is a proof of that. The heresies and schisms which have by degrees separated from Catholic society the entire Eastern Church and one half of the Western Church have sprung from no other causes. It is true that in the present state of society the declaration of these principles could not involve such grave consequences. The independence of civil society, which at other times might have been regarded as menaced by them, is now both in fact and by law beyond all controversy and all attack. Liberty of conscience and of religious belief being universally admitted,

z

renders it impossible to imagine even the domination of religious society over political society. We have nothing of that kind to fear. Those even who most vehemently urge the Council to convert this doctrine into a dogma admit that the necessities of the times will condemn such decrees to remain dead letters. Modern principles have been definitively adopted into the public law of Europe, and will never be erased from it, because they are indispensable alike to the dignity and the liberty of men and of Governments. It is no feeling of political uneasiness which influences us and dictates the representations which we feel it to be our duty to address to the Council. It is a fear at once more serious and more disinterested, the fear that there may be created—if the wisdom of the Holy See does not prevent it—a kind of antagonism between civil society and the Church, which may be equally prejudicial to both. The Government of the Emperor considers and has always considered these harmonious relations in the midst of Christian nations as one of the most essential bases of social peace. How can that be maintained if the highest religious authority of this world, that of the Œcumenical Council, should condemn the maxims upon which legislation reposes, and declare the principles of public law to be contrary to the principles inculcated by the Church? When the echo of such declarations issuing from the Vatican shall resound from the pulpit of the smallest village, and touch the conscience of the humblest Catholics, will there not be reason to apprehend that the germs of difference thus implanted in men's minds may be developed, and sooner or later be converted into real facts? The Government of the Emperor has yielded to the most imperious sense of duty in calling the grave attention of the Fathers of the Council to these dangers. As far as relates to itself personally nothing could have been easier than to have silently allowed these projected resolutions to be adopted, having always the power to declare null and of no effect every maxim opposed to the public law or to the general feeling of the French nation. Advice of this kind has not been wanting. The Government, however, has not hesitated for a single instant in repudiating these timid suggestions. The policy which consists in waiting till an evil be done, and has become incapable of reconsideration, is a short-sighted policy, and one which would not be worthy either of the Emperor or of a great nation like our own. Proved friends of the Church, it is not our place to recall the proofs of devotion to it which we have given. But we may say that we remain faithful to our traditions, and never shall we have rendered to it a more signal service than on the day when, addressing the august representatives of Catholicity assembled at Rome, we warn them of the danger to which they are exposing themselves. We do not desire to restrict their freedom; we only raise our voice in order to point out to them the consequences of their acts. We are towards them the faithful interpreters of public opinion everywhere expressed, which, far from remaining silent, speaks aloud and unmistakably. It is perilous to brave it, useful to consult it, necessary to listen to it. There would be an end of public peace, of the concord between political and religious society, if a reactionary movement should be excited in men's minds, and if the enemies of the Church were furnished with a weapon which they would know only too well how to use against it. The Cardinal Secretary of State, in replying to the communication which the Emperor's Government thought it right to make to him immediately upon the presentation of the *Schema de Ecclesiá*, has himself perceived the necessity of allaying the disquietude which the ideas contained in that document had everywhere occasioned. His Eminence, in his despatch of the 19th of March, speaking of the two powers, said 'that the competence of each being perfectly distinct and definite, according to the object for which each was established, the Church does not exercise by virtue of its authority a direct and absolute interference in questions relating to the constitutive principles of Governments, the forms of civil institutions, the political rights of citizens, the duties of the State, and the other points referred to in the note of the 20th of February.' Afterwards treating of the Concordat, Cardinal Antonelli again says that 'the points of mutual competency being settled by that document, any decisions which may be arrived at by the Council in respect of such matters will not in any way affect the special stipulations agreed upon between the Holy See and France and other Powers.' The Emperor's Government is far from undervaluing the importance of these declarations. It takes notice of them, and it derives from them great confidence in the definitive resolutions of the Holy Father and the Council. It is, in fact, by adopting the line of conduct marked out by the Cardinal Secretary of State that the apprehensions which we have expressed to the Holy See, and which we now submit to the august assembly itself, can be removed. It is by declarations based upon these wise maxims that the Fathers of the Council may return to that point of view from which public opinion, calm and sympathetic, but now anxious and alarmed, watched the completion of the grand task committed to their wisdom. It depends upon them to modify in this sense the propositions which have been submitted to them, and thus to avoid all declarations which would be of a nature to disturb and compromise the relations between the Church and the State. As the guardians of social peace, Governments have as a first duty to guard against aught that can affect it. They would be failing in their duty if under existing circumstances they maintained silence. The agitation caused in the Christian world by the expectation of the resolutions of the Council warns them of the imperious necessity of speaking out and of protesting against propositions which if they were adopted must inevitably produce grievous troubles. These propositions affect the State as much as they do religion, the Church, and the Holy See."

EXTRACT FROM A DESPATCH DATED VIENNA, MAY 10, 1562, ADDRESSED BY FERDINAND I., EMPEROR OF GERMANY, TO ANTON MÖGLITZ, BISHOP OF PRAGUE, HIS DELEGATE AT THE COUNCIL OF TRENT.

"WE have no wish to withhold our opinion on this important point, but on the contrary deem it incumbent upon us to declare, unreservedly, that in the Germanic Empire the acts and decisions of the Imperial Parliament are alone valid and lawful. There is no power on earth which can absolve any of the Prince Electors, Princes, or Estates from the duty of conforming to the constitutional decrees of the Imperial Parliament. It will therefore be advisable for the Fathers assembled at the Council to refrain from discussing the acts of secular authority, as vested in the Emperor and Imperial Parliament of the Holy Roman Empire of the Germanic Nation. Should they reject this advice and presume to condemn any acts of the civil power, they will find nobody to obey their behests, and only render themselves ridiculous (*ludibrio multorum*). Wherefore I charge you to offer the utmost resistance to any such intentions on the part of the Fathers, and to take care t' Imperial decrees and acts be repudiated or conde them."

The above shows that even three hundred yers when Catholicism was much more imposing than constituted powers of Germany objected to the infringement of their legitimate authority by the Pope. Nor were statesmen, however orthodox, in those early days disposed to shut their eyes to the very worldly means sometimes employed to obtain spiritual decrees from the Council. In another despatch to his Delegate, the same Emperor complains that the Council is frequently exposed to dictation and intimidation from Rome. "The enemies of the Catholic religion," he says, "have long been in the habit of insinuating, that the Holy Spirit is sent to the Council, from Rome, by relays of post horses (*per dispositos equos*)—a sarcasm which recent events have caused to be uttered with double pungency."

THE END.

www.ingramcontent.com/pod-product-compliance
Lightning Source LLC
Chambersburg PA
CBHW030319240426
43673CB00040B/1219